WHISPERERS

DANGEROUS & DEADLY TALKING

BISHOP M.B. JEFFERSON

WHISPERERS: Dangerous & Deadly Talking

Publisher: Scripture Music Group LLC
805 E Bloomingdale Avenue
Brandon, FL 33511
mbjeffersonministries.org

Credits:
Content: Bishop M.B. & Dr. Brenda Jefferson
Cover Designer & Graphics: Joseph Anthony
Layout & Editor: Cynthia Ahmed; LIVCC Staff

Your support and respect for the property of this author is appreciated.

NOTE: *All scriptures cited in this book are from the King James Version of the Bible unless otherwise noted.*

ISBN: 978-1-7365465-4-3

LIBRARY OF CONGRESS CONTROL NUMBER: 2021925633

ACKNOWLEDGMENT

I thank God for all of you reading this book.

I want to acknowledge my loving wife, Dr. Brenda Jefferson. Thank you for always helping me. I appreciate your words of wisdom and sustained support, through every obstacle and trial. I am thankful to walk this spiritual journey, hand in hand with you.

To all of my sons and daughters, both spiritual and in the natural, your support means the world to me. I pray this book continues to guide you and gives you insight, as you continue to lean on Christ and learn of Him.

A special thank you to all of the Overseer's & Ministers of W.A.F.I. (World Assemblies Fellowship International), Pastor Calvin, Pastor Ninkia, and all the first family on your servitude and continued faithfulness to the ministry.

INTRODUCTION

My greatest hardships in ministry, were a catalyst to a bright and victorious future with God. *Who knew?* Those grievous moments that tested my resolve, where I was at my threshold for pain, were the same moments that built my character and fixed my faith. I learned early on, *not only* about the power of the Word of God, but also the capacity of the words spoken out of my own mouth. Have you ever said something that you regretted later? Have you ever done something that went against your personal values? You didn't have to say it.. or even do it, but in your flesh and present state, you just couldn't seem to find different words to say.

My desire in sharing, ***Whisperers: Dangerous & Deadly Talking***, is to give insight to others on the delicacy of choosing your words, and wisdom on the harm they can bring. As ministers, we must give account for every idle word that we speak. Even more, we must suffer through hearing the unfiltered words of others, under our care and in our congregations. "Woe unto you, when all men shall speak well of you! For so did their fathers to the false prophets. But I say unto you which hear, Love your enemies, do good to them which hate you, bless them that curse you, and pray for them which despitefully use you" (Lk. 6:26-28).

Being able to discern different types of spirits, knowing those that labor among you, and giving grace for under-developed words, is part of the process required to be a good leader. New and mature believers alike, will stumble in their actions and speech. Our job is not to 'set them straight' or 'get them told,' but to help that person replace those jagged and arrowed words, with God's Word instead. "For the Word of God is quick, and powerful, and sharper than any twoedged sword, piercing even to the dividing asunder of soul and spirit, and of the joints and marrow, and is a discerner of thoughts and intents of the heart," (Heb. 4:12). Good leaders give people room to grow. They cultivate a heart of humility, knowing that only through God's power can truth and judgment lead others to repentance (Psa. 94:15).

Yes! **Holding the gospel, will at times require you to hold your tongue.** In the faith, we must be careful and on guard at all times. Any and *all* manner of sin can cause a believer to compromise their beliefs. **These minor vices can soon develop into a breach of spirit, and become a danger to the soul.** Dangerous words. Deadly sins. Surmounting obstacles. Lost opportunities. Distance and division. Thwarted blessings. Crumbling associations and damaged relationships. Deafening lies, whines, and whispers. So much trouble, surmounted from a few combined letters, from a single word. Or, simply from what you and I decided to say.

Behind the pulpit, we have a greater responsibility for our word choice, than most. What we give away and even the words we refuse to speak, have a potential impact on our members. **Have you ever heard the phrase, *"Don't shoot the messenger?"*** It is used to describe the act of revealing a difficult truth that a listener does not want to hear. This obstruction of consideration blocks the "good news" from penetrating bleeding hearts. It causes a person to hear a controversial message, bad news, or provoking words, instead of accepting what is truly being said (Acts 5:33). Unwilling to receive God's instruction, this then gives that individual unwarranted admonition, to blame the messenger. "Cry aloud, spare not, lift up thy voice like a trumpet, and shew my people their transgression, and the house of Jacob their sins," (Isa. 58:1).

Being in Christ's stead, we are ambassadors of Heaven, and our sole mission is to reconcile others back to God (2 Cor. 5:20). The right words can cause us to go higher, allowing us to see and hear on a different frequency. **Aligning and elevating our speech places us on a Heavenly channel. Speaking from the spirit sets us on a different network.** *Are your words in tune with God?* Use your words to uplift and draw others closer to Him. Remember, faith comes by hearing and hearing through the Word of God (Rom. 10:17).

The Holy Spirit must be the captain of your salvation, helping you to navigate and direct your communication the right way. You will not *like* or *agree* with everything that you hear. You must reject any rumor, falsehood, and/ or *whisper* that is contrary to what the Word of God says. Over time, I learned that backbiting, gossip, lies, and combatting the works of darkness came with the 'territory,' so to speak. Through trial and error, I became more mindful of my thoughts and in effect, my words presented in return.

Once I discovered the peace of God, the Word of God became a safe haven for me. The scriptures became my refuge. **I learned to speak without fear, exactly what God told me to say, exactly how He told me to say it.** A righteous boldness developed inside of me, to deliver the message...*precisely as it was sent.* You can't sugarcoat reality, and you can't make an ugly truth that God wants to reveal appealing. "But when they deliver you up, take no thought how or what ye shall speak: for it shall be given you in that same hour what ye shall speak," (Matt. 10:19). When I began to do this, I became a living witness of the signs and wonders of God. *I was amazed!* Miracle after miracle, testimony after testimony, deliverance and healing, breakthrough and blessings, all made manifest because I said what God told me to say. Obedience to the Word of God, is what unlocks incomprehensible and profound blessings in our lives. A life that honors God is built off of the truth.

For forty-five plus years in ministry, my wife and I, listened to the voice of God and followed His leading. We understood principles of faith, and by mirroring God's Word in our speech pattern, we began to implement it. Soon, we saw positive changes in ourselves and others. Many began to follow the call, becoming disciples of 'Book, Chapter, and Verse.' Through our various teachings, we continued to encourage Holiness, often illustrating the power of speaking from the spirit and not the flesh. It became common to hear Dr. Brenda Jefferson say, *"I'm Blessed and Highly Favored"* when offering a greeting. Listening to me bellow, *"Come on Outta Here"* when calling out devils in prayer, became the norm.

Still, in the beginning, people called me everything but a *child of God*. They characterized, my wife and I, as charismatic leaders with ill-intentions. From being a cult-like ministry, to money-hungry, to part of illegal activity, to mismanaging money, to benefiting from the poor, to neglecting those in our care. Various lies, media reports, bulletins, and misrepresented news directed at us, ultimately to distract us from our assignment of saving souls. Many targeted our family and loved ones, as they continued to work out their own salvation and seek God for themselves. "Do ye indeed speak righteousness, O congregation? Do ye judge uprightly, O ye sons of men," (Psa. 58:1).

Even so, we kept our hearts right. Together, we endured the persecution. Despite the dangers of moving forward and despite the temptation to quit, we continued to serve, build, and help those in need. Truthfully, our fear of disobeying God was greater than any fear of mortal men, political plays, or worldly consequences. "In God have I put my trust: I will not be afraid what man can do unto me," (Psa. 56:11).

Thankfully, God sustained us. We did not understand it at the time. *In the beginning, it was rough!* Even now, we still endure daily setbacks through which we must pray. Even now, we still fight an ongoing assault amongst folks words. In the midst of it all, we lift up our hands to Heaven and give God thanks. We hit our knees and cry out to God for protection, from every enemy against the purpose of God (2 Cor. 10:3-11). "No weapon that is formed against thee shall prosper; and every tongue that shall rise against thee in judgment thou shalt condemn. This is the heritage of the servants of the Lord, and their righteousness is of me, saith the Lord," (Isa. 54:17). I want to encourage you to let God be your defender. Be assured and confident that He has never lost a battle! Everything you are going through is *all* a part of His good plan.

Amid our struggles, it became apparent to all...*that God was with us.* Our numbers grew and our affiliated churches flourished. Despite the people who tried to damage our reputation, authoring articles, and stirring conflict, God kept us and expanded our territory. He melted limitations, shut many mouths, opened many doors, and softened hearts. Those who God assigned to us, knew our hearts and understood the vision. Through those trials, God was preparing us to deliver a nation. Through those trials, God was leading us to restore a generation.

God was calling us to *speak life* into those who surrounded us with danger, to love those who spoke evil of us in their conversations. Every time someone would try to kill us with deadly words, God would take us a little higher (Prov.

18:21). Every time we suffered risk or a loss, it eventually became a long-term profit or benefit. I share my testimony with you, only in hopes of building your faith.

As you read on, I pray that you search the chapters in expectation! I hope that you discover the voice of God, and that He would grant you the wisdom to lead you out of your troubles and into sudden miracles. **My prayer is that you never view your words in the same limited, ordinary, or insignificant sense again.** My prayer is that you will widen your perspective, speaking life and not death in the face of adversity. Let God's Word have its way! Talk big. Believe big. Love big. Allow God to increase your capacity today, and know that He has it all under control. Keep your mind stayed on Him and express your words... as He would. Elevate your mindset and make your proclamations to Heaven. Communicate your faith. Manifest your dreams. Walk in overflow and know that you serve *a real, real* BIG God.

TABLE OF CONTENTS

TABLE OF CONTENTS

1 TROUBLE TALK

As children, we learn our letters and alphabet at a young age. Understanding how to construct simple phrases and then sentences, sets us up for a lifetime of talk and communication. Our daily conversations and speech are an important component of our world, and who we are in it. Words can be intense, their power arising from our emotional responses when we read, speak, or hear them.

One word, in fact the *same* exact word, can hold a separate context, having multiple meanings to different people - in different places. For example, just say the word "fire" while barbequing at home, or in the workplace, or in a crowded theater, and you'll get three completely different but powerful emotional reactions. At the barbecue, hearing the word "fire" will send someone to check on the condition of the food: edible or crispy? At the workplace, hearing the word "fire or fired" may cause someone to start packing up their desk items, thinking they are no longer employed, or wondering 'who burnt the popcorn again in the lunchroom?' At a crowded theater, in hearing the word "fire," there may be a thunderous rush of the audience towards the exits for fear of an emergency.

The Bible itself is composed of over 750,000 words and a staggering three million plus letter characters. *It is the most important and influential text you will ever read.* Its words have profound power when spoken. Reading it, will give you indescribable strength, wisdom and knowledge. Knowing the truth will make you free, but speaking and doing the will of God, will keep you from the troubles of this life, and the blazes of hell in the next. "Herein is our love made perfect, that we may have boldness in the day of judgment: because as He is, so are we in this world," (1 John 4:17).

Mostly, we navigate our lives, build our relationships, and evaluate one another's actions based on our natural senses. Our interactions are mostly determined by what we see others do and by what we hear others <u>say</u>. **Our conversations create connection; they can cause laughs, invoke fear, bring tears, create intimacy, produce breakthroughs, and even make trouble (Matt. 12:25).** "Therefore thus saith the Lord, If thou return, then will I bring thee again, and thou shalt stand before me: and if thou take forth the precious from the vile, thou shalt be as my mouth: let them return unto thee; but return not unto them," (Jer. 15:19).

Spiritually-speaking, we seek to edify and uplift in our communication (1 Cor. 2:16). We listen to understand, but 'who really knows what is in the heart of an individual?' How do we say what we mean and mean what we say? How do we talk with certainty, but without offending? Or give life through our words, instead of promoting doubt, fear, or propagating unbelief?

God's Word contains so much knowledge on the power of your own words, and steering your speech in the right direction to make positive change (Heb. 4:12). There is a wise adage that says, "If you listen carefully enough, someone will tell you exactly what kind of person they are." If we don't intentionally control our dialogue, we can very easily find ourselves in unexpected situations, or in *big trouble*.

When hearing the word "trouble," many think of their children standing in the time-out corner, a student being punished in detention, a loved-one being ill, or a citizen breaking the law. **However, spiritual trouble arises when our speech contradicts spiritual laws and principles.** We land ourselves in big trouble *with God* when sin leaves our lips, and develops into a more pressing issue or circumstance.

When thinking over hardships and difficulties in our past, many of us will notice a pattern emerge. The cause of troubling circumstances set out from mindless words spoken, from the depths of a troubled heart. In effect, sin followed. "And He said unto them, why are ye troubled? And why do thoughts arise in your hearts," (Lk. 24:38). **A moment of troubled-talk can lead to a lifetime of upset, regret, heartache, disappointment, and negative situations**. Your words have power.

Ultimately, our words form the perceptions that shape our beliefs, drive our behavior, and eventually, create our world. For example, your relationship may have been different, if you did not say those damaging or hurtful words to your husband or wife. You may have gotten that promotion at work, if you would have kept your cool in the conference room when responding to your superior. As a child, you could have prevented punishment, by telling your parents the truth instead of lies. For some, you could have prevented jail-time, by choosing to avoid peer pressure, 'saying no' to unhealthy attachments and friendships.

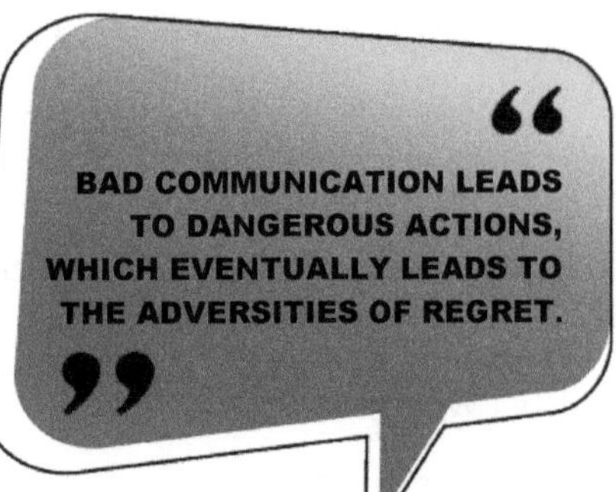

When we communicate ineffectively, we are more likely to find ourselves saying something inappropriate, something that will cause disappointment, something contrary to our values, something otherwise questionable. "Wherefore, my beloved brethren, let every man be swift to hear, slow to speak, slow to wrath," (Jam. 1:19). **Bad communication leads to dangerous actions, which eventually leads to the adversities of regret.**

A key component of "minding the mouth" is intentionally thinking before speaking. Most of us have heard this "think before you speak" concept since adolescence, but have lacked the spiritual understanding to implement it. Our words have the potential to destroy and create, heal and uplift, help and hinder, justify and condemn. Scripture teaches us that where there are many hurtful or hasty or negative words, that transgression is unavoidable. “In the day of my trouble I will call upon thee: for thou wilt answer me,” (Psa. 86:7).

In the faith, we should be people of measured speech, we should be known for being reserved when it comes to talking. When we are in our flesh, we speak the wrong things (Gal. 5:16-17, 25). **Idle chatter can lead to poverty and eventually lead to sin.** “In the multitude of words there wanteth not sin: but he that refraineth his lips is wise,” (Prov. 10:19).

The cost of *poor communication* is an expense much higher than most of us are willing to pay. Constantly berating and bad mouthing others, creates detachment in your relationships and transgression over time. Too much talk leads to trouble and gossip. Too much talk leads to comparison, negative attitudes, and discontent. Too much talk leads to lying and deceit. Too much talk leads to arguments, hurt feelings, and misunderstandings. Too much talk can even cause you to get a bad deal in a business transaction. “Keep thy foot when thou goest to the House of God, and be more ready to hear, than to give the sacrifice of fools: for they consider not that they do evil. Be not rash with thy mouth, and let not thine heart be hasty to utter any thing before God: for God is in Heaven, and thou upon Earth: therefore let thy words be few,” (Eccl. 5:1-2). **Some people talk too much and say too little.** We must direct our words in a positive direction, being based on the Word, and limit the unnecessary.

Here are some helpful tips to watch your words:

T – Take under consideration the truth

H – Have reasoning and understanding for what is being said

I – Inspire; intellectualize the need; stop and inhale

N – Needful; Is it necessary

K – Know the timing, be kind, kind-hearted

While communication in itself is not destructive, we must have restraint over the thoughts that we think, and the words that we choose to speak. **As a representative of God, others will listen to your language in an attempt to locate your heart.** Often, your core values and intentions are announced through your word choice. By recognizing ***trouble talk***, in ourselves and in others, each of us can make a substantial effort toward identifying these failings and preventing them from becoming a lifestyle of sin. These missteps will undoubtedly ruin our relationships and hinder our blessings. "Even so the tongue is a little member, and boasteth great things. Behold, how great a matter a little fire kindleth. And the tongue is a fire, a world of iniquity: so is the tongue amongst our members, that it defileth the whole body, and setteth on fire the course of nature; and it is set on fire of hell," (Jam. 3:5-6).

Filthy talk is dishonest and messy. The best fix for 'muddy speech' is to meditate on the Word of God. Learn to replace negative thinking with truth. **By possessing the mind of Christ, you can transform your words into a Heavenly language.** There is a time to be silent and a time to speak. God's Word is filled with the truth of who we are, who He is, and is full of supernatural power. When you consistently meditate on the scriptures, using them to fight off negative thinking, you limit corrupt communication (Prov. 23:7). *Yes!* The power of God is stronger than ANYTHING! **When you use His Word, as a weapon to fight the warfare against negative words, then you will find peace!** Rest in Him, and He will get your mind right. Look for the positive, and your words will begin to change.

When you retain God in your knowledge, you cannot be malicious in your talk, invent evil things, be full of deceit, debate, or judgement. Touch your neighbor and ask: ***"Are You a Whisperer?"*** A *whisperer* can be defined as a gossiper, a newsmonger, someone scandalous, a rumor-filled person, or a blab. Formally defined, it is someone who speaks very softly using one's breath without vocal cords, especially for the sake of privacy. Yet, do not be deceived, God is not mocked, whatever you sow, you will reap. *Do you privately whisper about your boss to your co-workers? Do you whisper about this friend - to that friend? Do you whisper about your spouse to your family? Do you whisper about your ex to your next? Do you whisper about your pastors or leadership in the church, to your brothers and sisters in the gospel?*

Recognize your pattern. Check yourself. Then, examine your conversations. Minor inconveniences can explode into major problems when hasty words are spoken. "And even as they did not like to retain God in their knowledge, God gave them over to a reprobate mind, to do those things which are not convenient; Being filled with all unrighteousness, fornication, wickedness, covetousness, maliciousness; full of envy, murder, debate, deceit, malignity; ***whisperers***, backbiters, haters of God, despiteful, proud, boasters, inventors of evil things, disobedient to parents, without understanding, covenant breakers, without natural affection, implacable, unmerciful: who knowing the judgement of God, that they which commit such things are worthy of death, not only do the same, but have pleasure in them that do them," (Rom. 1:28-32).

Toxic errors occur when we fail to bite our tongues, and let our natural urges take over and outcomes run their course. "Death and life are in the power of the tongue: and they that love it shall eat the fruit thereof," (Prov. 18:21). Our lips can snare our souls and deliver our destruction. **When contaminated and uncontained, our words can wound.** "A fool's mouth is his destruction, and his lips are the snare of his soul. The words of a talebearer are as wounds, and they go down into the innermost parts of the belly," (Prov. 18:7-8).

Dangerous devices lurk in the heart of someone who has no regard for their words. Your communication reveals your character, thus righteous words should be as deep waters, overflowing with good things, and being full of wisdom. *Hold fast to the faithful words that have been taught to you!* In discreet and chaste conversations, the sincerity and good works of your sound speech cannot be condemned.

A smart person knows what to say, but a wise person knows whether or not to say it. Affirm those things which you believe, being careful to hope for eternal life. We must be free from envy, malice, and hating one another. In a gentle and meek disposition, the love of God is made manifest; in our words, actions, and deeds (Tit. 3:2-9). "In all things shewing thyself a pattern of good works: in doctrine shewing uncorruptness, gravity, sincerity, sound speech, that cannot be condemned: that he that is of the contrary part may be ashamed, having no evil thing to say of you," (Tit. 2:7-8).

In salvation, we should not be brawlers, striving against the law, or deep in contention. We must avoid foolish questions and be intentional in what we speak. "That the communication of your faith may become effectual by the acknowledging of every good thing which is in you in Christ Jesus," (Phil. 1:6). **Malicious and deadly words are flawed, imprecise, counterfactual, unfitting, mistaken, improper, inaccurate, unreliable, faulty and untrue.** Truth is delivered through meekness. It is through humbleness and sincerity, that we can compel others to know our God and embrace our beliefs. British poet, George Herbert once said, "Good words are worth much, and cost little." Your words have value. "But let it be the hidden man of the heart, in that which is not corruptible, even the ornament of a meek and quiet spirit, which is in the sight of God of great price," (1 Pet. 3:4).

Think about your own big life-lessons. How did you learn them? Experience is the best teacher. Decide to keep out of trouble, by changing your language and adjusting your attitude. Every day you unintentionally cultivate your character, by what you allow through the gates of your ears, and through the gates of your eyes. "Whoso keepeth the commandment shall feel no evil thing: and a wise man's heart discerneth both time and judgment," (Ecc. 8:5). ***Are you setting a Godly example?*** It takes practice, but the Holy Spirit is a helper. You can start today by noticing the good in bad situations. Also by, expressing gratitude regularly and complimenting others. Work through negative emotions to practice mindfulness, cultivating compassion and bouncing back from challenges.

Words are extremely powerful tools that can uplift our personal energy and improve our lives. Though, we're not often conscious of the words that we speak, read, and expose ourselves to, they have significant impact on our choices and mannerisms. Don't let people pull you away from God. "Be not deceived: evil communications corrupt good manners," (1 Cor. 15:33). *Evil communication* is generally being in contact with an ungodly thing, an ungodly person, or an ungodly group of people. Yes, even the words of others can easily affect our mood. In these situations, meditate on the Word of God (Ecc. 7:21). Use it as a means to refresh, renew, and wash your mind in faith-stirring principles to shift how you feel. Soon, you will find yourself *speaking* these positive truths that you have read aloud.

When you speak God's Word, you are reinforcing your faith and changing the atmosphere in your home, and your surroundings (Rom. 10:8). A famous adage by actor Robin Williams says, "No matter what anybody tells you, words and ideas can change the world." Negative attitudes and words, feelings of helplessness and hopelessness, can lead to physical signs of chronic stress. These "bad vibes," as some say, hinder our influence and repel others away. Negativity too, can become a habit. Various health articles explain that frequent criticism, cynical thoughts, and denial can create neural pathways in the brain, which encourage frequent sadness. These negative tendencies can cause our brain to distort the truth and make it even more difficult to break this negative cycle of thinking.

Many of us tend to utter pessimistic, harsh words against ourselves when we get disappointed or when we fail at something. Negative self-talk is exactly what it sounds like: talking to yourself in a negative, or mean way. We often tell ourselves things that we would never say to a loved one or a friend. Dialogue such as, "my hair looks stupid today," or "I can't do anything right," or "things will never change for me," or "no one likes me," are all contrary to faith-filled speech. These internal and unfitting self-assessments can demoralize your confidence in God, and influence your life in a negative way. Instead, fill your mind with positive affirmations that align with God's Word. For instance, it that says we are fearfully and wonderfully made; the head and not the tail; a chosen generation; and heirs of promise.

Breakthrough begins by acknowledging setbacks and adjusting. **God isn't in love with the future you. He loves "you" right now, as you are and where you are.** Shift full-force ahead into a better life. Build better talk by moving towards Godly change. Pursue a version of you that reflects Christ, even if it requires breaking off old pieces of yourself that are no longer recognizable, and altering words that no longer fit. "Therefore if any man be in Christ, he is a new creature: old things are passed away; behold, all things are become new," (2 Cor. 5:17). Before you speak, do a mental filter of your words, to see if they reflect Christ. If your emotions are running "hot," take a step away and close your lips until you cool down. Take a moment to block that anger and frustration, by replacing those thoughts and words with good substitutions (Jam. 3:2-8). Allow your words to reflect the consistency of what you know, and not how you feel in the moment when you are angry.

Changing your talk and developing good habits is a process. Yet, the product of a controlled tongue, is time well spent. Trouble and strife usually follow an unruly person who cannot discipline what they feel, or control what they say (Jam. 3:8, 10). It is said that even quiet people have loud minds, processing and observing the world around them, then waiting before making a response. While confidence is *not always* silent, insecurities *are often* loud. Being still, quiet, or at peace is not just a state of mind, but a conscious effort to live, speak, and act as Christ has instructed.

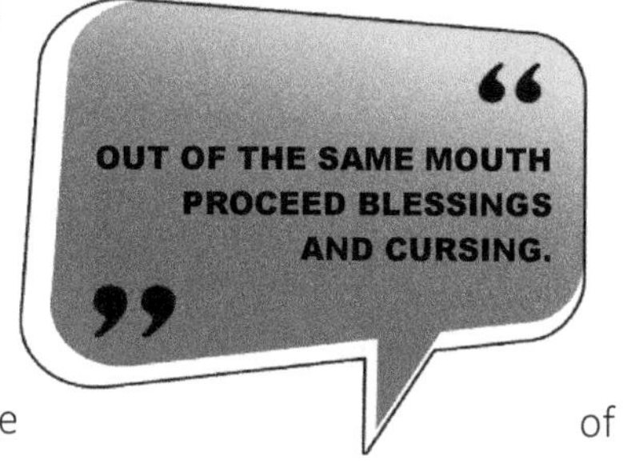

Out of the same mouth proceed blessings and cursing. *Yes!* A lion handler tames a beast, but who can tame the tongue? We must continue to be authentic in our shortcomings, allowing God to lead. Here are some helpful ways to limit trouble-talk. You can honor your truth while being considerate. Try and decipher what is important and unimportant information that the other person should know, then identify what your purpose for communication is. When we are thoughtful about our message, considering how our words might make another person feel, we express ourselves better.

Below are practical phrases, and godly suggestions on how to respond in different situations. You must guard your heart and guard your mind when interacting with others. These examples can be used to manage and navigate difficult conversations:

SCENARIO ONE

AN UNCOMFORTABLE SITUATION WITH A FRIEND *OR* LOVED ONE:

- "I'd prefer not to answer, it is none of your business."
- "That should not concern you."
- "It's a complicated situation and I don't think it's appropriate to discuss the details at this time."
- "I don't appreciate you speaking to me that way."
- "I don't think it's best to talk about this right now. Things will work out; have faith."
- "I think this conversation is heading in the wrong direction."

SCENARIO TWO

FACING PEER-PRESSURE *OR* AVERTING A CRIMINAL ACT:

- "Officer, things are not as they seem. I mean well."
- "No, I don't think this is right for me. I have changed my mind."
- "I'm going to head back, it's getting late."
- "Things are getting out of control"
- "I think we need to head out."

SCENARIO THREE

WORK CONVERSATIONS *AND* AVOIDING GOSSIP:

- "____ is really trying. I think its best that we try and help them instead of talking about them. What can we do to influence him/her in a positive way?"
- "If we don't agree with the way ____ does things, or have a suggestion that can make things better, we should tell ___ our concerns directly."
- "I have a suggestion and wanted to bring it to your attention."

When in doubt on how to respond or what to say, silence or removing yourself from the conversation is always the best option. In unavoidable situations, don't be afraid to pray and ask for God's guidance. The Holy Ghost is a helper. Avoid half-truths, be direct, but don't allow the conversation to go in a direction that could lead to trouble. Sin, deceit, backbiting, or lying usually occur when people are fearful, or are not comfortable with where the conversation may be headed (Prov. 16:13). Remember, everyone asking questions is not entitled to answers. "Whoso keepeth his mouth and his tongue keepeth his soul from troubles," (Prov. 21:23).

Take action to avoid trouble and live peacefully with others. Honesty is always the best policy. *Watch your thoughts, mind your words, and change your world.* "Commit thy works unto the Lord, and thy thoughts shall be established," (Prov. 16:3). If you are struggling in this area, find ways to practice effectual communication and improve your talk with others. Start by saying thank you, articulate expectations, provide meaningful information, avoid assuming, and don't spin messages (Prov. 28:23). Remember, good communication is a skill, and like all skills, it takes practice and feedback to get better.

SCRIPTURE SUMMARY

Psalms 86:7

Proverbs 10:19

Proverbs 16:3, 13

Proverbs 18:7-8, 21

Proverbs 21:23

Proverbs 23:7

Proverbs 28:23

Ecclesiastes 5:1-2

Ecclesiastes 7:21

Ecclesiastes 8:5

Jeremiah 15:19

Matthew 12:25

Luke 24:38

Romans 1:28-32

Romans 10:8

1 Corinthians 2:16

1 Corinthians 15:33

Galatians 5:16-17, 25

Titus 2:7-8

Titus 3:2-9

Philemon 1:6

Hebrews 4:12

James 1:19

James 3:2-8

James 3:8-10

1 Peter 3:4

1 John 4:17

CHECK YOUR UNDERSTANDING

1. A *whisperer* is someone who speaks very softly, using one's vocal cords for the sake of privacy, with malice intent.

   (True) **(False)**

2. What scripture mentions "a whisperer"? __________

3. Which scripture references sound speech as unable to be condemned, preventing others from speaking evil of you?

   (a) Titus 2:7-8

   (b) Proverbs 18:7-8

   (c) Philemon 1:6

4. Death and life are in the power of the __________.

5. Which scripture explains the value of a meek and quiet spirit?

   (a) James 3:5-6

   (b) 1 Corinthians 15:33

   (c) 1 Peter 3:4

6. What scripture says when you keep your tongue, you keep your soul from trouble? __________

7. Out of the same mouth proceed blessings and __________.

2 VOICE OF HOPE

Satanic influences are seeking an entry point into our lives - through slander, rumors, and gossip. The spiritual confinement that results from negative communication, becomes the chains and shackles of this lost and dying world. Those who cling to false liberty, adopting the lies of a failing nation, and absorbing the misinformation of a troubled generation; walk senseless, blind, and hard-of-hearing. We must control our mouths and monitor our speech.

Do you delight in digging up "dirt" on other people? Do you find pleasure in persuading other people not to like someone? Are you most comfortable when you are counting others out? We have all had flashing moments where we may have uttered something, mumbling under our breath or aloud, then afterwards thought "I shouldn't have said that." Iniquity, troubled talk, and foul language are bondage in the life of a believer. Backbiting constitutes as hidden sin. If you do not address the person directly, those private and harmful words directed in malice towards someone else can become problematic. It spreads like fire. "And withal they learn to be idle, wandering about from house to house; and not only idle, but tattlers also and busybodies, speaking things which they ought not," (1 Tim. 5:13).

Refuse to give place to the devil. Decide to shape your speech to build, and not tear down. "Put away from thee a froward mouth, and perverse lips put far from thee," (Prov. 4:24). Don't grieve the Holy Spirit by the way you live, communicate, or with how you conduct yourself. *Grieve* means to cause great distress; to mourn, shed tears or suffer, even ache. Then further, it is described as a painful wound causing devastation. To grieve the Holy Spirit is to crush, to sting, to sadden, or even upset. Don't use foul or abusive language. Be careful using slang, cease from speaking profanity. In all of your efforts, seek righteousness in sincerity, being concerned about disappointing God.

Discern and self-evaluate the tendencies that are holding you back. Mentally tough people realize that they possess an active part in how they control their thoughts, behaviors, and consequently their outcomes. The choice is always yours. ***You*** choose the words that you speak. ***You*** choose the thoughts that you think. ***You*** choose to act in certain ways or to do certain things. More than anything else, we have to keep desiring Holiness, pursuing righteousness and developing Christ-like character. "Keep thy tongue from evil, and thy lips from speaking guile. Depart from evil, and do good; seek peace, and pursue it," (Psa. 34:13-14). *Guile* is defined as being sly, or cunning, with schemes, ploys, double-dealings, and deceit. Seek God's presence everyday by spending time with Him! When the mind is renewed, a new attitude activated, and new practices can begin. Righteousness and true Holiness rest upon your heart. Righteousness can be defined as being honorable, virtuous, and morally right. Our words mean nothing, if our actions are the complete opposite.

Act according to what you believe. Danger dwells in the midst of devious words. When your mind is filled with the love of Christ and the fullness of God, it is free from the deceit of this world. "(9) Wherewithal shall a young man cleanse his way? By taking heed thereto according to thy Word... (11) Thy Word have I hid in mine heart, that I might not sin against thee... (15) I will meditate in thy precepts, and have respect unto thy ways (16) I will delight myself in thy statutes: I will not forget thy Word," (Psa. 119:9, 11, 15-16). **Your words are the most inexhaustible source of insight or injury, intelligence or ignorance, death or a potential catalyst to your dreams.**

Be a stronger version of you by allowing God to penetrate the layers of your heart. When you live life in the present, you also increase your mindfulness, and most importantly you stop overthinking. Silence the incessant inner voices that re-play in your head, and turn down the mental chatter. When you live for God and abide in His Word, it is impossible for wrong words to depart from your lips, or even wrong thoughts to cross your mind. **Wrong words linger in the minds of those they offend. They find habitat, make a home and wait, to send you to hell.** "A man shall eat good by the fruit of his mouth: but the soul of the transgressors shall eat violence. He that keepeth his mouth keepeth his life: but he that openeth wide his lips shall have destruction," (Prov. 13:2-3). *Are your words digestible? Do the contents of your speech nourish or aggressively deplete?*

Build yourself up by praying in the Holy Ghost (Jude 1: 20). Pray continually about the small things, not just occasionally about the big things. *Focus on flourishing.* Australian writer, Markus Zusak is quoted saying, "The best word shakers were the ones who understood the true power of [their] words. They were the ones who could climb the highest." When your mindset is in a different place, the contents of your mouth must shift. A Heavenly mindset leads to angelic words. Be bold and be brave in speaking the Word of God, truth has no bounds!

"WHEN YOUR MINDSET IS IN A DIFFERENT PLACE, THE CONTENTS OF YOUR MOUTH MUST SHIFT."

May you have the audacity to break the patterns in your life, which are no longer working for your good. The discipline to speak truth without fear, starts with getting rid of any negative residue in your mind. When the enemy constructs a web of deceit, God will allow any opposition to fall into the very traps that they have set for you. "Thou art snared with the words of thy mouth, thou art taken with the words of thy mouth," (Prov. 6:2). Corrupt communication entangles, becoming a spiritual stronghold for those who fall prey or become entrapped. This habituation pattern of wrong thinking is built into one's thought life, and then expressed vocally.

What do your words express? What kind of picture are they painting? Are they conveying depression, recurring unbelief, a bad temper, lust, resentment, verbal abuse, or failure? "Let no corrupt communication proceed out of your mouth, but that which is good to the use of edifying, that it may minster grace unto the hearers. And grieve not the Holy Spirit of God, whereby ye are sealed unto the day of redemption. Let all bitterness, and wrath, and anger, and clamour, and evil speaking, be put away from you, with all malice," (Eph. 4:29-31). If you find yourself in a place of torment, God wants to release you, but the key to your prison is in your own hand.

SPIRITUAL PRISON

Sin is like prison. In this state, many are captive, not physically but in their hearts and minds. The worst kind of "miserable" is one where you are unable to explain why, and if you did – no one would be able to comprehend your unhappiness. People try all sorts of things to overcome their feelings of imprisonment, but only Jesus' blood can truly cleanse our sins and set us free. "Remember them that are in bonds, as bound with them; and them which suffer adversity, as being yourselves also in the body," (Heb. 13:3). Although many believers don't realize it, God has given each of us a "get out of jail free" card. His intentional sacrifice on the Cross, made it possible for us to escape the shackles of sin, and death.

The truth is - we were all guilty of something, and Jesus dropped the charges!

Judge: "How do you plead?"

Defendant: "Guilty, your honor."

What is spiritual prison? Imagine a place of containment, confinement, a repetitive reminder of your failures and shortcomings. A place of isolation, dark and empty, a lifeless pit of regret, despair, and heartache. Spiritual prison is a place of mental captivity, a holding place for people arrested in the spirit by the adversary (Lev. 24:12). Bound and unable to get free. 'Prison' is not only seen in the scriptures as a social institution but a spiritual reality, a tormented holding space before judgement, even identifying it with the power of death. A place that traps the soul and holds you captive. In this state of iniquity, your thoughts, words, and actions are contrary to right, embodying works of evil. "Wherein I suffer trouble, as an evil doer, even unto bonds; but the Word of God is not bound," (2 Tim. 2:9).

As you begin to evolve spiritually, you begin to notice the toxic nature of certain relationships, places, and associations. **Some individuals cover up vile hearts with accessories, cologne, filters, new threads, and makeup, but have ugly hearts, ugly souls, and ugly actions.** Beware of self-sabotaging behaviors. Are you in a continuous loop of avoidance to mask the real problem?

Uncontrolled worry, doubt, overthinking, and fear often sound like cruel and mean words.

7 Signs of Spiritual Imprisonment:

- Being Fearful and Unbelieving
- Not Forgiving the Past; Holding Grudges
- Being Stuck in an Unhealthy Relationship
- Using Corrupt Communication and Language
- Not Being Authentic, or Standing in your Truth
- Obsession with Television, Porn, and Social Media
- Choosing to Stay Depressed and not Asking for Help

Unforgiveness, depression, sinful speech, and unhealthy attachment is a rope that secures and interlocks you to everything of the past. It becomes a thorn of pain, abuse, and self-neglect that cripples your spiritual growth. "I went down to the bottoms of the mountains; the Earth with her bars was about me for ever: yet hast thou brought up my life from corruption, O Lord my God," (Jon. 2:6). Forgiveness is never for the other person; it is for you to move past the wall of grief blocking you from your release. Release yourself from people-pleasing, misdirected desire, wrong words, and inordinate affection. It will lift a heavy burden off of your shoulders. "The Lord is good, a strong hold in the day of trouble; and He knoweth them that trust in Him," (Nah. 1:7). God not only sees where you are, He sees where you can be. If you don't see your worth, no one else will either. Christ values you, not based off of your performance or your actions, but simply because of who He is!

Fear, anxiety, negative thoughts and self-imprisonment always begin in our hearts and minds. Open the gate of your heart, to allow the light of Christ to flow freely. Breakthrough any lack of compassion and wrong thinking that is limiting your healing, and hindering your faith. "For I know that in me (that is in my flesh,) dwelleth no good thing; for to will is present with me; but how to perform that which is good I find not. For the good that I would I do not: but the evil which I would not, that I do. Now if I do that I would not, it is no more I that do it, but sin that dwelleth in me. I find then a law, that, when I would do good, evil is present with me. For I delight in the law of God after the inward man. But I see another law in my members, warring against the law of my mind, and bringing me into captivity to the law of sin which is in my members. O wretched man that I am! Who shall deliver me from the body of this death?" (Rom. 7:18-24).

God's Word is the only thing that can illuminate you. Truth is the only thing that can set you free. Yet, a person dull of hearing, cannot interpret righteous words. Their deafness has separated them from God, they go astray working wickedness, and speaking lies. "Their poison is like the poison of a serpent: they are like the deaf adder that stoppeth her ear," (Psa. 58:4). In order to be a *voice of hope*, you must be first partaker to hearken unto the Word of God. Those individuals who hear and see not, dwell in captivity; thus the law of liberty is not able to be released from their mouths. "For this people's heart is waxed gross, and their ears are dull of hearing, and their eyes they have closed; lest at any time they should see with their eyes, and hear with their ears, and should understand with their heart, and should be converted, and I should heal them. But blessed are your eyes, for they see: and your ears, for they hear," (Matt. 13:15-16).

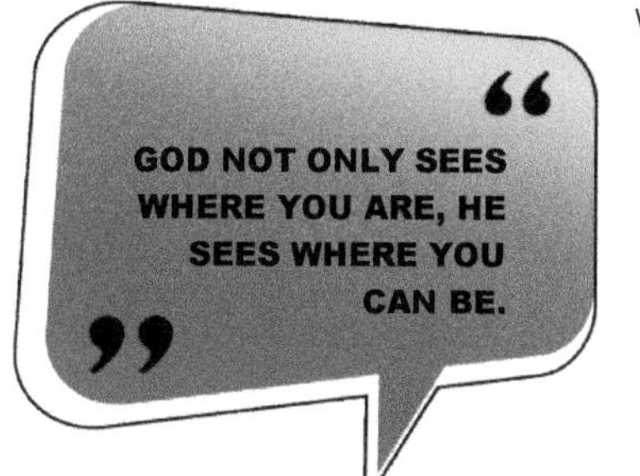

You are going to make it! It is a great comfort to know that we will never have to face anything on our own. "For the Lord heareth the poor, and despiseth not his prisoners," (Psa. 69:33). His love and peace give us the strength to keep moving. The endurance to keep praying and the faith to praise Him, in spite of what we are going through, is the tiny spark that make all the difference in our lives. It sets us on fire... for Him. **You can be overlooked, talked about, ridiculed, laughed at, mocked, plotted against and still come out on top.** We serve a God who can move mountains in moments, but sometimes everyday miracles are simply good people, with kind hearts. God isn't asking you to figure it all out, He is asking you to speak faith words and trust that He already has!

The good news is that Jesus Christ died on Calvary, that you and I may walk in total freedom, complete victory, escaping the clutches of misery and despair. The captivity of 'doomed dialogue' is no match for the hope-filled truth of the Bible. Freedom and hope are available to you today through the Word of God. He is relentless in pursuit of your heart. He wants to change you from the inside-out. He wants to restore you, make you over, and give you a new song.

God is your hope, when you have nowhere to turn. God is your guide, when life gets dark, and the fog of uncertainty surrounds you. God is the one who compels your heart to know Him, when the pounding cycle of pain and problems seem unbearable. When life incapacitates you, and you are clinging to life, the Son steps in to redeem you. **Jesus Christ is your hope, your deliverer, your healer, your lawyer, your credit, your redeemer, your shield, and your salvation.**

Accordingly, when you move, live, and breathe in Him, you become as the mouth-piece of God. As a reflection and representative of Heaven, we are always on assignment (Acts 17:28). **Nevertheless, our eternal messenger of hope and an enduring token of love, *is* perfection at the cross.** Jesus is the sustaining example of hope, life, and liberty. Think on Him. Accept His mercy. Bask in His grace. Then, talk about His goodness.

The Lord is our rock, our fortress, and our deliverer. Only He can release those who sit in those dark dungeons in their mind. "The Lord also will be a refuge for the oppressed, a refuge in times of trouble," (Psa. 9:9). Some strongholds build up a stockpile of thoughts that become a breeding ground for awful word selection. A *stronghold* can keep a believer from hearing good news. It can keep a person from thinking clearly, accepting the truth, and changing for the better. The Word of God possesses supernatural power to break every stronghold over your life! The stronghold of selfishness, lust, lies, and greed have been broken.

When you give Christ the key to your heart, He unlocks every stronghold that has kept you constrained. His grace releases wisdom, strength, and honor. He enlightens your life with optimism, and faith, and positivity to believe for greater, and to trust in the supremacy of His power. Through Him, we can change our confession and embrace true salvation. It first starts with a desire to change, and a sincere word spoken. You no longer have to be a slave to sin, you no longer have to serve your flesh (Rom. 6:6). **Deliverance lies in your mouth.**

Think about it. How many times has your communication been contrary to what you need? How often have you allowed wrong thoughts to deflect into inaccurate language, soon becoming a crutch to your goals? How many times have you used the words, ***"I'll be happy when..."***

- I'm Married / In A Relationship
- My Business Succeeds
- I Get that Promotion

- I Lose that Weight
- I Have More Money
- I Get that Job
- I Have Friends who Understand Me
- I Fulfill God's Purpose For My Life
- I Travel the World
- I Start a Family
- I Get that Degree
- I Overcome this Addiction

When your happiness, contentment, or well-being is contingent on someone or something else, you give away all of your authority to a source or person that you have no influence over. This is a *mental trap* that leaves you feeling powerless. Control what you can control. The only thing we have control over is ourselves: our mind, our decision, our speech, and our own actions. **Accept the failures of yesterday, recognize obstacles that might arise tomorrow, but speak life into the possibilities of today.**

Often, we have a tendency to let our circumstances defines our character, and weigh us down. When we do this, we use our present conditions as an excuse to restrict the future success that we want, or hinder the happiness we desire to obtain. Instead of giving undue credence to the brick walls and external circumstances that may surround you, take into account your strengths, seek possibilities, draw closer to God, and practice optimism. Influential American author, Dale Carnegie has a famous quote that states,

"Happiness does not depend on any external conditions; it is governed by our mental attitude." Two people can look outside the same 'prison bars,' one seeing mud the other seeing the stars: one visualizing hope and the other impending defeat.

Resilient people, those who are mentally tough, understand the power that they have over their own decisions and their words. Christ-centered people, those who stand on the Word of God, understand the power of their confession and are determined to be the best that they can be, in Him. "But what saith it? The word is nigh thee, even in thy mouth, and in thy heart: that is, the word of faith, which we preach; That if thou shalt confess with thy mouth the Lord Jesus, and shalt believe in thine heart that God hath raised him from the dead, thou shalt be saved. For with the heart man believeth unto righteousness; and with the mouth confession is made unto salvation," (Rom. 10:8-10). God will never make you look ashamed. There is no condemnation in Him (Rom. 8:1).

On the cross, Jesus bore all of your fears, guilt and shame so that you don't have to bear them any longer! So many people are being tormented by their past; by their failures and mistakes, or by the ways they've been victimized by another person. You can enjoy freedom by resting in His Word! "And you, that were sometime alienated and enemies in your mind by wicked works, yet now hath he reconciled. In the body of His flesh through death, to present you Holy and unblameable and unreproveable in His sight," (Col. 1:21-22).

Once you grasp this truth, you'll not only be free from the jailhouse of your past, but also be free to go forward and experience a new beginning in Him. Whoever shall call on the name of the Lord *will* be saved. Former President of South Africa, Nelson Mandela once said, "There is no passion to be found playing small – in settling for a life that is less than the one you are capable of living."

If you continue in the faith grounded and settled, and are not moved away from the hope of the gospel, you can live a blessed life. *What does freedom mean to you?* Right! Stand firm, and do not let yourselves be burdened again by the yoke of bondage. Dwelling on the cares of this world can choke your hope, and draw your sights down to an "earthly" level, with carnal reactions and fleshly responses. It is God's grace that increases our capacity to love, to have joy, to experience peace, and to enjoy life. God has given us incredible promises. If you are running low on hope today, turn to the Bible to recharge. "Beloved, now are we the Sons of God, and it doth not yet appear what we shall be: but we know that, when he shall appear, we shall be like Him; for we shall see Him as He is. And every man that hath this hope in him purifieth himself, even as He is pure," (1 Jn. 3:2-3).

Hope leads to faith. It is having strong confidence in the face of doubt. It delivers courage, strength, and boldness - instead of fear. Hope can clothe an impatient soul with endurance, when everything else around them is enticing them to quit, when everything is falling apart. Hope can cause an individual to get a second wind – to not get discouraged, to not give up, or give in because they have something to keep going for, something to keep hoping in (Heb. 6:19). It is the anchor of our soul.

To have *hope* is to want an outcome that makes your life better in some way; to cherish a desire with anticipation. It encourages us to look forward, despite the odds. When you envision a better future for yourself and your family, it motivates you to take the steps needed to make it happen. *Faith says it is so now, and hope says in the future... it could happen.* **Hope is the final objective, a possibility capable of being achieved.** Our ultimate hope and desire is to make it into Heaven. Do you want to go, or do you have reservations about where you are going?

The Lord delights in those who fear Him, those who place their hope in His unfailing love. *Will you trust God, in spite of your past trauma?* May the God of all hope fill you with so much joy and peace, so much faith and wisdom, that your trust overflows in Him. People are fickle and their compassion is often limited. When your enemies chase you sore, a stone of suffering weighing you down, call upon His name in the low dungeon, and He will hear your voice (Lam 3:51-57). Though you may have to endure grief, suffering, affliction, lack, and heartache... *there is hope*. Hope believes you will get through it. It remembers the times you made it through before, and believes that God can do it again. "This I recall to my mind, therefore have I hope. It is of the Lord's

"PEOPLE ARE FICKLE AND THEIR COMPASSION IS OFTEN LIMITED."

mercies that we are not consumed, because His compassions fail not," (Lam. 3:21-22). Great is His faithfulness! Let us lift up our hearts with our hands, to the Heavens!

Prayer is an eager hope that something good will happen. You are capable of being a *voice of hope* in the midst of these chaotic and uncertain times. With God, you can lead others on the pathway of finding Jesus. Someone needs you to help them through the darkness. They need a plan, an aspiration, a possibility or expectation to hold on to during times like these. Someone needs you to tell them that things can get better, they need you to reconcile them back to God. Others need you to introduce them to who God is. Through your struggles and testimony, someone is recognizing that they too, can have hope. They are recognizing that if God did it for you, He can do it for them too.

We all desperately need courage during hard times. You can deepen your faith in God by realizing that you don't just need to "cope," but you can actually be free. Know that one bad day is not the end of the world. Ask questions to gain clarity, always pray for understanding. See the good! Remember, you are facing challenges, not problems. Feel the emotions, but do not allow them to determine your destiny. Don't let perfect be the enemy of good. You are making progress with every subsequent step that you take. Your faith is growing with each trial that you make it through.

Think of your spiritual growth, similar to levels on a video game. God has designed that specific obstacle course or test with your weaknesses, preferences, and temptations in mind. With each level that you pass, conquering the trials and tribulations of that season or "level," you gain a little more wisdom and power to continue on to the next. If you don't successfully learn the lesson or pass the test on that particular stage, you continue to recycle the same situations. Until you have the faith to effectively make it through the course, overcoming the difficulty and learning the lesson, situations will continue to linger and repeat. Once you successfully make it through, then God can elevate you higher and higher in Him.

God is maturing your faith, not just through hearing the Word of God, but by way of actual setbacks and learning experiences. As you proceed to higher heights or deeper depths in God, you will find more traumatic obstacles to overcome. You will encounter various situations, that you have yet to encounter that will require you to seek His guidance and ask for wisdom. **New levels, new devils**.

Nevertheless, stand firm in the midst of adversity. Be ready for the battle, and stay armed with spiritual weapons to win the war. *"Choose your fighter,"* as they say in the virtual world. Pick a side... God's way or the world's way? We can't determine our opponents, but we can choose our defender. So, choose your fighter for this level or this season that you are in. Who do you prefer to fight this battle on your behalf? Who do you believe can open up the prison doors in your life and set you free? What person do you believe can defeat every adversary in your life? I don't know about you, but I choose – Jesus. *His moves, His strength. His power, His plan. His spirit, His way.*

As you release your burdens, and overcome your fears, your faith is getting stronger and stronger. In order to develop deep convictions and cultivate a deep relationship with God, you must put His Word in your heart, so that righteous words can be released from your lips. **Talk is cheap when you don't value what you say.** When Christ remains at the center of your life, everything else revolving around it seems to find its own way, falling into its proper place.

Today, we do not know the battles of tomorrow or what the future may hold. We do not know the thoughts that may try to take us captive on the next day, or the words that we will want to say, thereafter. All we can do is hope in the God who holds us and guides us, each and every day. All we can do, as believers, is become a light and an inspiration to those who have lost their way. All we can do, is stand firm in the liberty, whereby Christ has made us free, and be a *voice of hope* for somebody else looking to be free.

SCRIPTURE SUMMARY

Leviticus 24:12

Lamentations 3:21-22

Lamentations 3:51-57

Nahum 1:7

Psalms 9:9

Psalms 34:13-14

Psalms 58:4

Psalms 69:33

Psalms 119:9,11,15-16

Proverbs 4:24

Proverbs 6:2

Proverbs 13:2-3

Jonah 2:6

Matthew 13:15-16

Acts 17:28

Romans 6:6

Romans 7:18-24

Romans 8:1

Romans 10:8-10

Ephesians 4:29-31

1 Timothy 5:13

2 Timothy 2:9

Hebrews 6:19

Hebrews 13:3

1 John 3:2-3

2 Corinthians 5:17

Jude 1:20

CHECK YOUR UNDERSTANDING

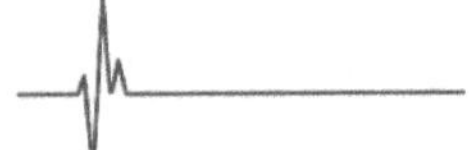

1. Satanic influences are seeking an entry point into our lives through slander, gossip, and rumors.

   (True) **(False)**

2. What is guile? ______________________

3. Which of these is <u>not</u> a sign of spiritual imprisonment?

   (a) Being fearful and unbelieving

   (b) Using corrupt communication

   (c) Being a *voice of hope*

   (d) Holding onto unforgiveness

4. Our eternal messenger of hope and an enduring token of love is ______________________.

5. Which scripture recalls the Lord's mercies as a reason to hope, explaining that His compassion do not fail?

   (a) Romans 8:1

   (b) Hebrew 6:19

   (c) Lamentations 3:21-22

   (d) Colossians 1:21-22

6. What scripture says, "The Word is night thee, even in thy mouth, and in thy heart, that is the word of faith, which we preach?"

   (a) Jonah 2:6

   (b) Romans 10:8

   (c) Psalms 69:33

7. A *stronghold* can keep a believer from hearing good news, accepting the truth, and changing for the better.

   (True) **(False)**

8. *Other people* choose the words you speak, the thoughts you think, and how you decide to act.

   (True) **(False)**

9. Talk is ______________ when you don't value what you say.

10. This chapter compares spiritual growth to ______________.

3 WISDOM WORDS

Imagine a care-free mouse, searching for food. Popping in and out of small crevices, holes, and walls, starving for something to eat. All of a sudden, it catches a whiff of dairy, the well-known aroma of cheese fills its nostrils, and off it goes in the wind. On the hunt for the next crumb of satisfaction. Then suddenly, SWOOSH! BAM! All you hear is a loud squeal in panic. The device door closes shut, and the mouse circles about looking for a way out. All to discover it has been caged on every side, captured with no way out.

As in this example, every day we are ***trapped*** by the destructive words that we choose to say, or set free through the use of wisdom words. "Thou art snared with the words of thy mouth, thou art taken with the words of thy mouth," (Prov. 6:2). A *"snare"* can be a trap or tool to catch birds or small animals. Yet, in a similar way, scripture compares the content of our words and the delivery of our message, as being powerful enough to capture, seize, or take.

While saying the right things can liberate; wrong words can lure, tempt, deceive, and cause harm to others. We can cultivate a lifestyle of Holiness by being inspired by the Word of God, and then choosing impactful words that will leave others inspired too. We have to keep working, desiring Holiness more than anything else, and pursuing Christ-like character. Pursuing righteousness means that we are a consistent work in progress, constantly pressing towards the mark. Our speech is perfected over time, through our obedience and our desire to reflect Christ. We must work on it every single day by spending time in the Word of God. "The way of the wicked is an abomination unto the Lord: but he loveth Him that follow after righteousness," (Prov. 15:9).

Wisdom is knowledge, as well as the capacity to make great use of it. "The tongue of the wise useth knowledge aright: but the mouth of fools poureth out foolishness," (Prov. 15:2). We must consciously choose wisdom and pursue it. Spiritual wisdom is not just about knowing what is good for us, or what is acceptable to say, but applying that knowledge into our everyday lives. It is the quality of having experience, understanding, and good judgment. Irish playwright George Shaw once said, "We are made wise not by the recollection of our past, but by the responsibility of our future."

Human wisdom is flawed and limited, however divine wisdom is open and limitless. "The fear of the Lord is the beginning of wisdom: and the knowledge of the Holy is understanding," (Prov. 9:10). Being good and moral is not enough – we must be wise. It is a transforming and illuminating light to do what is just, right, and fair, in the face of evil. To speak wisdom, your mind must be filled with the love of Christ. To experience the fullness of God, your mind must be free from the deceit and the idolatry of this world.

True Holiness causes you to take on a new attitude, to become righteous in your talk, and to cleanse your ways. "That He would grant you, according to the riches of His glory, to be strengthened with might by His Spirit in the inner-man. That Christ may dwell in your hearts by faith; that ye, being rooted and grounded in love, May be able to comprehend with all saints what is the breadth, and length, and depth, and height; And to know the love of Christ, which passeth knowledge, that ye might be filled with all the fulness of God," (Eph. 3:16-19). God is able to do more than we can ask or think, yet we must seek the knowledge found in His Word.

How many times did you know what you should say, and spoke something different? How many times did you know what you should have thought and supposed a different idea? Wisdom does not always equal common sense, it also *not* the same thing as knowledge. An individual can be acquainted with facts, truth and principles, but when that information is not applied to their own life; it's just knowledge. Wisdom will require you to act on that information, and speak with understanding. Words of wisdom possess soundness, insight, and discernment. "If any man defile the temple of God, him shall God destroy; for the temple of God is Holy, which temple ye are. Let no man deceive himself. If any man among you seemeth to be wise in this world, let him become a fool, that he may be wise," (1 Cor. 3:17-18).

The wisdom of this world is foolishness with God, He taketh the wise in their own craftiness. Strive to be a person of value by becoming a reflection of His Spirit. Be someone who recognizes challenges and chooses to do something about them. Be someone who gives a kind word to someone in need. Be someone who looks for the good in bad situations. Rational speech is not necessarily logical or sharp, but it is sound. Surround yourself with wisdom by staying near wise counsel. Learn from your mistakes. Chaplain and activist, Gail Masondo once said, "Discernment prevents experience from being your teacher." Watch and observe, so you do not have to learn great lessons of pain through suffering.

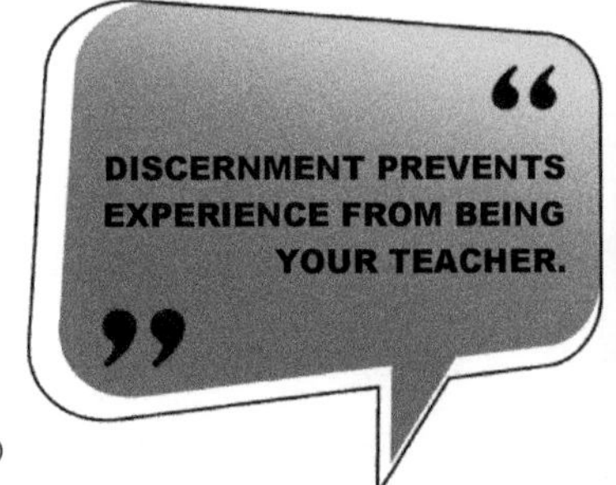

What you learned yesterday was yesterday. Remind yourself that every minute, is a new opportunity for life to continue to teach you. Be open to learning new things as you evolve. A collection of biblical principles and sound speech will be added to your life, once you are willing to become a student. Through God's Word your eyes are enlightened, and as a result the content of your character and words will change. "The eyes of your understanding being enlightened; that ye may know what is the hope of

His calling, and what the riches of the glory of His inheritance in the saints," (Eph. 1:18). When our lips no longer know what to ask for in prayer... *God hears our heart.*

Words of wisdom involve talking to Jesus daily. Tell Him what made you smile today. Tell Him about your goals. Tell Him about your favorite things. Tell Him your secrets. Tell Him what you're confused about. Tell Him what you're anxious about. Tell Him why you're trusting Him. Tell Him why you're grateful. Tell Him what you love about His creation. Tell Him how He has blessed you and give thanks through your prayer! "A man hath joy by the answer of his mouth: and a word spoken in due season, how good is it!" (Prov. 15:23).

Today is a great day to speak good things! Your life is found in Christ. You can rise up from anything. "Set your affection on things above, not on things on the Earth. For ye are dead, and your life is hid with Christ in God," (Col. 3:2-3). God can completely re-create your life! You are not stuck, you have choices. You can think new thoughts and create new habits. You can speak uplifting words and learn something new. You can decide to move forward into who God has called you to be, and never look back. Once old practices are done and gone away, old words cease and sinful behaviors end. Then, you then become a new creature in Christ (2 Cor. 5:17). Embrace this newness of spirit, as you declare His miracle-working power.

IRON SHARPENETH IRON

Various elements have different meanings throughout scripture. In the Bible, an *iron rod* of metal is used to describe power and strength. "And out of His mouth goeth a sharp sword, that with it He should smite the nations: and He shall rule them with a rod of iron: and He treadeth [with] fierceness and [the] wrath of Almighty God," (Rev. 19:15). Wisdom will allow you to build the Kingdom of God with like-minded individuals. No one is alone, there are mutual benefits through sharing ideas, following leadership, and mentorship. **We make ourselves better through maximizing each other's strengths and building on each other's weaknesses.** "Iron sharpeneth iron; so a man sharpeneth the countenance of his friend," (Prov. 27:17). When we frame our words to knit together and not tear apart, we make each other better.

A leader is only as good as their team. A *blacksmith* is someone who sharpens dull metal on a blade's edge, so that a new edge is formed. The 'sword of the spirit' *is* the Word of God. It is a discerner of what we want to say, and how we intend for it to sound when communicating with others. "For the Word of God is quick, and powerful, and sharper than any twoedged sword, piercing even to the dividing asunder of soul and spirit, and of the joints and marrow, and is a discerner of the thoughts and intents of the heart," (Heb. 4:12). People who are good for your soul, talk from a place of compassion, and do not leave you with feelings of regret. Nothing kills hope quicker than evil communication. Nothing feels heavier than words left unsaid.

It is important to build our spiritual vocabulary, so that our words do not cut or harm others in a negative way. We can sharpen others mindfully by providing clear expectations, speaking vision and possibility to people, building genuine relationships, engaging in honest conversations, sharing the credit, praising in public and correcting in private. Remember, speaking the truth does not give consent to talk hate, or crush someone's confidence – unless those words of reprimand or direction are spoken by leadership (Isa. 58:1). For teammates, speaking the truth in love allows other's to filter that content through their spiritual ear. We must listen long enough to process what is being said, and if it agrees with our inner-man, we must be open enough to receive that criticism and correction without grief.

> "WORDS OF WISDOM INVOLVE TALKING TO JESUS DAILY."

Team players have the heartbeat of their leaders. They display servanthood and a willingness to help build the vision of the church. Understanding the nature of a *team player* requires establishing the meaning of a "team." A team is considered to be any group of people brought together to accomplish a particular goal. They **share** the same goals, **agree** on how to accomplish the same goals and are able to **work together** to achieve the same goals. Being a part of a team builds character, teaches empathy, and ultimately achieves objectives. Group effort is more effective than individual effort. "Two are better than one; because they have a good reward for their labour," (Ecc. 4:9).

From a Biblical standpoint, *teamwork* means sharing in biblical responsibilities based on biblical goals, values, priorities, giftedness, training and God's leading for the ministry. A member of a team must have the ability to work well with others who have different personality styles, motivations, and opinions. Through cooperative collaboration, a team member can adapt to change, be transparent, and put aside personal agendas to be mission-conscious. Whatever the case may be, each team has a leader, who must make final decisions and set the ultimate vision for the organization. *Where no counsel is, the people fall: but in the multitude of counsellors there is safety.*

American author, Robert Ludium once said, "Blessed are the flexible, for they shall not be bent out of shape." While we cannot control everything that is happening in the world today, let alone everything that is happening in our own lives, we can be disciplined in how we respond and interact with others. "Wherefore laying aside all malice, and all guile, and hypocrisies, and envies, and all evil speakings," (1 Pet. 2:1). Communicative team players do not isolate themselves from the group, they understand that there is strength in union and open communication. This is why God tells us to be anxious for nothing, and to stay in prayer. We are not to be proud, boastful, or speak with a "stiff-neck" when engaging in dialogue (Psa. 75:5). As a team, we should be seeking to *complete* each other, not *compete* with each other. We must be intentional about operating with integrity and humility, as we pursue individual assignments and Kingdom goals together.

Evil speaking gives place to the devil, and invites Him into your residence, whether it be your spiritual-house or God's building. For instance, if you leave your home and the windows are open, the door is unlocked, and the alarm is off; you are inadvertently inviting burglars into your house to rob you. Similarly, if you are not careful to watch your thoughts and examine your words, you are opening up your spirit to an all-out assault from the enemy. This enemy of your soul only comes to bring destruction into your life. "The thief cometh not, but for to steal, and to kill, and to destroy: I am come that they might have life, and that they might have it more abundantly," (Jn. 10:10).

The easiest way to destroy an organization is to cause it to become divided against itself. Be conscious not to kill your brothers and sisters in Christ with your words. Be careful not to harm your teammates and separate relationships with your mouth. **Remove yourself from gossip, because the same people who talk about others *to you*, will turn around and talk about you *to others*.** "Wherein they think it strange that ye run not with them to the same excess of riot, speaking evil of you," (1 Pet. 4:4). Your team or fellow-members should be a safe place to share and socialize, free from backbiting and evil speaking.

Negative words and negative thinking can choke your blessings. You must shut every door, close every window, and seal every crack to prevent disruption and defeat. Use wisdom with your words to prevent bitterness, hostility, outrage, complaining, and resentment in ministry and in the workplace. "A noise shall come even to the ends of the Earth; for the Lord hath a controversy with the nations, He will plead with all flesh; He will give them that are wicked to the sword, saith the Lord," (Jer. 25:31).

When God brought you into the ministry, He made room for your gifts. He called you into salvation for a greater purpose and assigned you a job or task, that only you can do. Allow Him to show you how to exercise your talent in collaboration with others, that there be no division among the church, and no assignment unfulfilled, wherein we can be an example to other believers. **The more we learn about Christ, the more we can walk in love and talk - just like Him.** *"But ye have not so learned Christ; If so be that ye have heard of Him and have been taught by Him, as the truth in Jesus: that ye put off concerning the former conversation the old man, which is corrupt according to the deceitful lusts; and be renewed in the spirit of your mind; and that ye put on the new man, which after God is created in righteousness and true Holiness. Wherefore putting away lying, speak every man truth with his neighbour: for we are members of one another. Be ye angry, and sin not: let not the sun go down upon your wrath: neither give place to the devil,"* (Eph. 4:20-27).

Words can light fires in the minds of men, acting as containers of faith or fear. You can make the decision to use wisdom with every word that you choose to say. “The words of a man’s mouth are as deep waters, and the wellspring of wisdom as a flowing brook,” (Prov. 18:4). You can be Kingdom-minded and use your words to build, uplift and not tear down. What wisdom can you find that is greater than kindness? Small changes and daily progress can lead to big results.

SCRIPTURE SUMMARY

Psalms 75:5

Proverbs 6:2

Proverbs 9:10

Proverbs 15:2, 9, 23

Proverbs 18:4

Proverbs 27:17

Ecclesiastes 4:9

Isaiah 58:1

Jeremiah 25:31

John 10:10

1 Corinthians 3:17-18

2 Corinthians 5:17

Ephesians 1:18

Ephesians 3:16-19

Ephesians 4:20-27

Colossians 3:2-3

Hebrews 4:12

1 Peter 2:1

1 Peter 4:4

Revelations 19:15

CHECK YOUR UNDERSTANDING

Down:

1. 2 ____ 5:17 mentions becoming a new creature in Christ.
3. Ecclesiastes 4:9 says ______ are better than one.
4. _____ words and _____ thinking can choke your blessings.
5. Proverbs 27:17 says "Iron sharpeneth iron, so a man sharpeneth the countenance of his ______."

Across:

2. The wisdom of this world is ______________ with God.
6. We must work on our speech everyday by spending time in ______________.
7. The words of a man's mouth are as deep _____ (Psalms 18:4).
8. A leader is only as good as their ________.
9. Words of ___________ possess soundness, insight, and discernment.

4 SPEAK LORD

The voice of the Spirit is ever calling us to relationship and transformation in Christ. As your relationship with God deepens, you learn how to recognize His voice. He speaks to us every day through scripture, and we in return, can communicate with Him through prayer. As we search for the solutions to life's afflicting situations, seeking for change, and growing our faith, we often find ourselves waiting patiently in a hope-filled silence, that God will come through for us.

As we listen for His voice, we have an earnest hope that He will speak. It may not be through a loud boom or a thunderous roar, but a soft whisper in a moment of a reflection. He may use a song, a sermon, a dream, or a word from a stranger to speak hope and direction into our lives. "Give ye ear, and hear my voice; hearken, and hear my speech," (Isa. 28:23). God's presence and His voice changes everything. We serve a living God who is always speaking to us through creation, through His Holy Bible, and through His Spirit. The process of hearing His voice requires, **(1)** first that He is speaking to us and **(2)** second that we are listening. "Whom shall He teach knowledge? And whom shall He make to understand doctrine? them that are weaned from the milk, and drawn from the breasts. For precept must be upon precept, precept upon precept; line upon line, line upon line; here a little, and there a little: For with stammering lips and another tongue will He speak to this people," (Isa. 28:9-11).

No matter your level of understanding regarding salvation or His Word, trust that God <u>*does*</u> want to communicate with you. We are all either positively or negatively influenced by what we hear, see, speak, and the actions of those around us. It is so important to take heed and listen, to absorb and process, *then* speak. We are all like sponges, and as we learn and meditate on the Word of God, it fills those missing areas of our countenance with good and righteous things.

Every syllable that you speak, every verb that you assemble, and every phrase that you articulate has the power to transform. Or it contains the possibility of holding your dreams hostage. Ask yourself: *What is really holding me back? What have I been taking in and <u>talking</u> out? What have I been absorbing and releasing into the atmosphere?*

What you *want* is biased, and limited, and often based on what YOU see. Yet, the positive shift that you *need* is purposeful, and Holy, and based on what God said. Blessings are your portion when you speak the right things. Invite Him in through worship and prayer, then prepare your heart for a mighty move of God. He speaks to us every single day. His solutions and His answers ultimately brings peace, deliverance, and victory in our lives. His truth and declarations rise up like tidal-waves on the inside, and then graciously spill over into every area of our lives. Saturate your vocabulary with truth and activate the Holy Spirit's power within you. "(9) Wherewithal shall a young man cleanse his way? By taking heed thereto according to thy Word... (11) Thy Word have I hid in mine heart, that I might not sin against thee... (13) With my lips have I declared all the judgments of thy mouth... (15) I will meditate in thy precepts, and have respect unto thy ways. (16) I will delight myself in thy statutes: I will not forget thy Word," (Psa. 119: 9, 11, 13, 15-16).

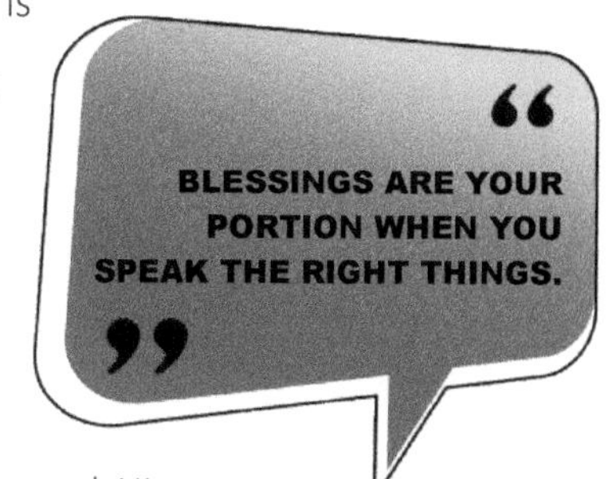

The authority of God is settled in Heaven. His truth can quicken and make alive, mend broken hearts and restore all those who are hurting. Ultimately, your knowledge and relationship with God, will set the tone for every other relationship in your life. **When He speaks, do not hesitate to do what you are called to do.** Don't tip-toe around His instructions waiting on acceptance to move. Simply take the step. GO! Everyone will not understand. Part of hearing His voice is realizing that not everyone will applaud, not everyone will approve, not everyone will celebrate, not everyone will support, not everyone will stay, not everyone will encourage, but in the end "people" don't have to "get it." No matter what the doctor says, the lawyer says, he says, she says, or they say... **If God said it, that settles it!**

God's voice is supreme. It doesn't obsess over problems, it doesn't gossip, it never contradicts scripture, and will always speak to your heart. Our circumstances do not change who God is. May you no longer be weighed down by the negative words and reduced expectations of others. Cancel them and return them back to the sender. Speak God's goodness over yourself and believe in possibility, instead. "The lip of truth shall be established for ever: but a lying tongue is but for a moment. Deceit is in the heart of them that imagine evil: but to the counsellors of peace is joy," (Prov. 12:19-20).

No word from God will ever fail. Cast down any false proclamations that have been spoken over your life in the past. Perhaps, it was a parent who said you'll never amount to anything, a teacher who said you're unteachable, an ex who said you'll never find love, or a superior who said you won't succeed. Don't allow your life to be a product of pessimists. Don't allow your spirit to be affected and neglected by naysayers. Command every curse spoken over you and your family to break, in the name of Jesus. Command every idle word, to be subject to the vision and provision of God. The mouth of fools will ingest foolishness, and only the heart of those that have understanding will seek knowledge (Prov. 15:4, 14).

A good word from God makes you glad, while contention, contempt, reproach, shame, bitterness, perversion, and idolatry will cause you to err with your lips. "Even a child is known by his doings, whether his work be pure, and whether it be right. The hearing ear, and the seeing eye, the Lord hath made even both of them," (Prov. 20:11-12). Hear the words of the Lord today! *He is speaking to you, are you listening?*

There is nothing greater or more compelling than the power of God. *Nothing!* It doesn't matter what the doctor says. It doesn't matter what the credit bureau says. It doesn't matter what the banker's report says. It doesn't matter what the news says. God *is* and *will always be* in control. When He speaks, His commands take form and multiply throughout the Earth. His words manifest and take shape to create, moving as an expression being sent back and forth on assignment. "For as the rain cometh down, and the snow from Heaven, and returneth not thither, but watereth the Earth, and maketh it bring forth and bud, that it may give seed to the sower, and bread to the eater: So shall my Word be that goeth forth out of my mouth: it shall not return unto me void, but it shall accomplish that which I please, and it shall prosper in the thing whereto I sent it," (Isa. 55:10-11).

Trials may come. Winds may blow. Weapons may be formed. Yet, YOU *can* have victory over it all. Hold on to Him in the midst of your tests. Hold on to Him in the midst of contrary words. Declare miracles in faith and settle yourself on His precepts. "No weapon that is formed against thee shall prosper; and every tongue that shall rise against thee in judgment thou shalt condemn..." (Isa. 54:17). When God speaks, it breaks mountains and topples hills. Those who gather together to work iniquity, spewing vicious venom with their lips and backbiting from their tongue, will utterly be taken by their own devices. The Lord will blow coals of fire against the wicked, and establish the outcast through His everlasting covenant and kindness.

When you keep your heart pure and you trust in the Lord, you will go out with joy and be led forward in peace. We manifest outwardly a reflection of what our inside contains. Harsh, critical, impatient, and irritated responses require us to practice patience. Recalling the grace that has been given to us, allows us to give grace to others. Maybe you went through hardship and suffering and survived, just so you could help someone else make it through. In frustrated moments, take time to give ear to what is really being said, and listen for the source of the confusion. The righteousness of God is revealed from faith to faith. Discipline yourself to stop absorbing the pain of other people, which is directed towards you through sharp words. Recognize that the way you live, listen, and treat other people is an everyday decision.

> "WHEN GOD SPEAKS, HE DOES IT WITH AN EXCLAMATION POINT."

When God speaks, He does it with an exclamation point! Marvelous things take place at the sound of His voice. When His presence enters a room and starts to move, every knee must bow, and every tongue must confess that He is Lord. Begin to adjust your speech to change your circumstances. When you think Holy, you can talk Holy. When you elevate your thoughts, you can elevate your language. **When you think bigger, you can speak better.** Every day you can tap into God's supernatural provision and blessings by emulating the Word. Replicate what it says out of your mouth, and then take action to do what it says to do. Initiate Godly language through book, chapter, and verse. By placing the scriptures on the inside of you, your spirit man takes hold to replicate and repeat. "Forasmuch as ye are manifestly declared to be the epistle of Christ ministered by us, written not with ink, but with the Spirit of the living God; not in tables of stone, but in fleshly tables of the heart," (2 Cor. 3:3).

Learn how to tap into greater things in your life, by examining yourself and taking accountability for various areas that you may have fell short in communicating. Sometimes, it's *easy* to say how we feel in a fit of frustration or in a moment of anger. Rather, than to act and speak on what we know and believe. Challenges are an opportunity for change. "All scripture is given by inspiration of God, and is profitable for doctrine, for reproof, for correction, for instruction in righteousness," (2 Tim. 3:16).

Hamza Yusuf once said, "Don't ever diminish the power of words. Words move hearts and hearts move limbs." Progression and improvement, require constraint and self-awareness. God has empowered you to adapt to whatever comes your way, be willing to continuously transform and take on new habits. Together, we can continually strive to get better. We become Ambassadors for Christ, when we practice what we are hearing. Tell your neighbor: **Do it,**

like you hear it. Then, say it like you mean it. Speak faith words and declare what *thus* said the Lord! "So then faith cometh by hearing, and hearing by the Word of God," (Rom. 10:17).

PARABLES IN THE BIBLE

Throughout history, God has initiated communication with humanity by speaking audibly. Many of the miracles that took place throughout scripture, were based on a word spoken by our Savior.

- ***An Angel Troubles the Water:***

The man at the pool of Bethesda was unable to enter the water, with no one near to help him get his healing. Seeing his physical struggle to receive deliverance, Jesus said to him with compassion, *"Wilt thou be made whole? ...Rise, take up thy bed, and walk,"* (Jn. 5:5-9). Jesus did not have to touch or lay hands on him. All He did was speak. Immediately, the paralyzed man experienced a miracle, simply through the power of Jesus' spoken words.

- ***The Ram in the Bush:***

God directed Abraham to take a journey. In his obedience and without having clear direction, he went into the land of Moriah to offer a burnt offering. I can imagine Abraham preparing mentally for the possible heartbreak of having to sacrifice his only son. In obedience, Abraham continued to follow instructions. As Isaac laid upon the altar of wood, Abraham lifted up his knife to kill him when suddenly he heard a voice. The angel of the Lord called out to him from Heaven saying, *"Lay not thine hand upon the lad, neither do thou any thing unto him: for now I know that thou fearest God, seeing thou hast not withheld thy son, thine only son from me."* Instead, a ram caught in the thicket appeared miraculously, as God provided a sacrifice for the burnt offering in the stead of his son (Gen. 22:1-18). God's voice was the source. His command is what made a way for the provision.

- ***Peter Walks on Water:***

On a ship in the midst of the sea, during a torrential storm, another miracle takes place. Jesus steps out of the boat and walks on top of the sea. Fearful and afraid, the disciples questioned what they were seeing. He then beaconed them to join, even telling Peter to *"Come."* That one word spoken by God, manifested a miracle. As Peter came down out of the ship, and despite his physical limitations, he actually walked on top of the water to go to Jesus (Matt. 14:24-32). Incredible! This is an example of learning to listen to the right voice. When Peter listened to the crowd, he began to focus on the wind and his doubt caused him to sink. Yet, when he focused on God and his words, he did the impossible.

You can make the impossible possible too! You must speak like you are victorious, speak like you are an overcomer. Impact the Kingdom by imparting into others that same revelation and power of God, through what you say.

You must speak victory if you want to live in victory. "But I say unto you, that every idle word that men shall speak, they shall give account thereof in the day of judgment. For by thy words thou shalt be justified, and by thy words thou shalt be condemned," (Matt. 12:36-37).

We are constantly in need of a Word from the Lord. Through a posture of listening, we can call upon God and humbly wait, listen, and hear from Heaven. Seeking direction prevents us from making mistakes. Having an ear to hear is what causes real change. "If my people which are called by my name, shall humble themselves, and pray, and seek my face, and turn from their wicked ways; *then will I hear from Heaven*, and will forgive their sin, and will heal their land," (2 Chron. 7:14). Use your words to heal, pray, and bring deliverance. Victory and prosperity lies within you.

SCRIPTURE SUMMARY

Genesis 22:1-18

2 Chronicles 7:14

Psalms 119:9, 11, 13, 15-16

Proverbs 12:19-20

Proverbs 15:4, 14

Isaiah 28:9-11, 23

Isaiah 54:17

Isaiah 55:10-11

Matthew 12:36-37

Matthew 14:24-32

John 5:5-9

Romans 10:17

2 Corinthians 3:3

2 Timothy 3:16

CHECK YOUR UNDERSTANDING

1. "All scripture is given by inspiration of God and is profitable for doctrine, for reproof, for correction, for instruction in righteousness" is found in 2 Timothy 3:16?

   (True) **(False)**

2. Blessings are your ________ when you speak the right things.

3. Which 'Parables from the Bible' are discussed in the Chapter where miracles took place based on the Word of God?

   (a) Angel troubles the water

   (b) Ram in the bush

   (c) Peter walks on water

4. If God said it, that ________ it.

5. Which scripture compares the words sent from God, as rain and snow that comes down from Heaven?

   (a) Proverbs 15:14

   (b) Isaiah 55:10-11

   (c) 2 Chronicles 7:14

6. By your words you are ________ and by your words you are ________ (Matthew 12:37).

5 SEASONED SPEECH

Have you ever had a flavorless meal? Steak with no salt, chicken with no pepper, macaroni with no cheese? Bland and tasteless, these nutritious entrées are not desirable or savory without being seasoned and well prepared to consume. This concept of adding spice and flavor to our natural food, can also be translated to our everyday speech habits. "Let your speech be always with grace, seasoned with salt, that ye may know how ye ought to answer every man," (Col. 4:6).

Our words, as believers, must be digestible and gracious. Speaking with *grace* means your words are wholesome, fitting, kind, purposeful, complementary, gentle, truthful, loving, and thoughtful. The speech of the new man must be sent to edify and have a positive effect on the hearer who listens. Our conversations should influence reflection in others, preventing corruption and filthy talking from engulfing the discussion. Purity of mind and heart will cause purity of language. **Seasoned speech will always say the right thing at the right time.**

One of the key words in this passage of Colossians 4:6 is the emphasis on the specific word "LET." In order to ***let***, we must be willing to change what we really want to say, to content that represents Christ well. This means we have to allow, permit, authorize, grant, empower, and sanction the scriptures to have dominion over the door of our lips. Having excellent speech is not about being false, unnatural, or deceitful, but about putting on a new spiritual wardrobe. We have to choose righteous talk, being compelled and motivated to flavor our words. Speech filled with *grace* cannot be formed based on what we think the hearer "deserves," but spoken as a blessing towards others, undeserved benevolence that could never be earned and is freely given. "A word fitly spoken is like apples of gold in pictures of silver," (Prov. 25:11).

Courteous, respectful, and patient conversations should be a pleasant experience for all that are involved. Structure your words in Holiness, trying not to be obnoxious, pushy, or argumentative, even in conversations that involve a difference of opinion. Wise words guide an interaction by adding insight, understanding, and are founded on Biblical direction. *Are your words of substance? Is your speech purposeful and of good use?* The daily offering of our words, should include flavors of faith, being interesting, memorable, satisfying, uplifting, and attracting other unbelievers.

Godly words and a positive attitude can even preserve health. While sinful words have a way of rotting the mind and the spirit. "The lips of the righteous feed many: but fools die for want of wisdom," (Prov. 10:21). Purity of speech reflects purity of heart, and impure language reflects unclean character. The fear of the Lord prevents us from having a forward tongue and destroying our neighbor. In the same way, a just tongue is valuable and is a way of life for those that keep instruction. Scripture teaches us that blessings are upon the head of the just and He will not suffer the righteous soul to be famished. "The lips of the righteous know what is acceptable: but the mouth of the wicked speaketh forwardness," (Prov. 10:32). As believers, we have an everlasting foundation when we frame our words on the Word of God.

The words of the Lord are pure, tried in a furnace of fire and purified. Then, sent to preserve the Godly man from the wicked. Many speak proud things with flattering lips, speaking vanity to their neighbor, and lies to the oppressed. Yet, true believers understand that their words are not their own, they are a direct reflection of Christ within them. "(2) They speak vanity every one with his neighbour: with flattering lips and with a double heart do they speak...(4) Who have said, with our tongue we will prevail; our lips are our own: who is lord over us?" (Psa. 12:2, 4). **Ask yourself today:** Who is Lord over my mouth? **Declare:** "My lips are not my own."

When others imagine mischief and gather together for trouble, our prayer should be for God to hear the voice of our supplication in the day of adversity. "...(3) They have sharpened their tongues like a serpent; adders' poison is under their lips...(4) Keep me, O Lord, from the hands of the wicked; preserve me from the violent man; who have purposed to overthrow my goings... (7) O God the Lord, the strength of my salvation, thou hast covered my head in the day of battle... (11) Let not an evil speaker be established in the Earth: evil shall hunt the violent man to overthrow him," (Psa. 140:1-13).

God searches the hearts of His people. Only He knows our objectives. He understands our thoughts and is acquainted with our ways. He knows every word of our tongue, yet being unperfect, fashions them altogether (Psa. 139:4). In tribulation and warfare, we want God to come to our aid. When we cry out to Him, we want Him to hear our voice in times of need. When we incline our hearts to do good and refrain from evil, keeping our eyes on the Lord, our words should be sweet like honey. When the upright call upon His name, He will not leave our soul's destitute, but will come to our rescue. Give thanks!

As believers, we should echo this prayer, "Set a watch, O Lord, before my mouth; keep the door of my lips," (Psa. 141:3). Don't allow the salt of our words to sting a wound, or to rub flesh, but allow it to add flavor to the conversation. God allow us to be ready to rescue and influence with our words. They remove stains, promote wellness, eliminate mess and odors, express tolerance, rather than judgment, and extend grace. The goodness of God leads others to repentance, and the inward circumcision of the heart will prevent our tongues from transgressing (Rom. 2:4).

Every day that we choose to speak vile contempt to others by mismanaging our words, we change the truth of God into a lie. Dissatisfaction, grumbling, and complaining keep us stuck in offense and prevent us from being thankful. We can demonstrate grace when we make allowances for the frailties of others. When in a group and you see the conversation going downhill, re-direct it in another direction. **Sometimes, we talk and forget who is listening.** The conversation extends beyond who we are speaking with, and we must remind ourselves that "whatever is coming out of my mouth, is coming out of my spirit."

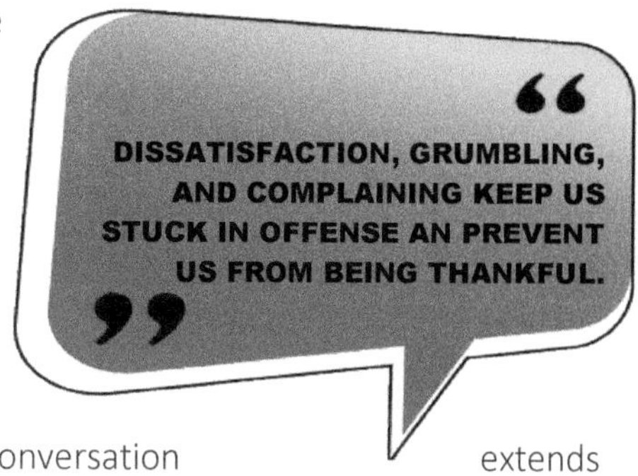

Can you smell what your words have been cooking? Deteriorating conversations leave behind a stench, or foul odor. God's Word teaches that we are to a sweet-smelling aroma in His nostrils. "For we are unto God a sweet savour of Christ, in them that are saved, and in them that perish," (2 Cor. 2:15). We must seek divine direction for wisdom regarding what we say. As believers, we are not to be messengers of corrupt things, lack, or death, but messengers of life.

Your words have great impact, and are probably more influential in people's lives than you realize. The content of your communication can bring death to a dream, a blow to one's faith, or get someone excited about purpose. Your words should give a boost and energize. What can you do to become the kind of person that people stop and listen to, every time you open your mouth to speak? "(1) Moreover, brethren, I would not that ye should be ignorant, how that all our fathers were under the cloud, and all passed through the sea,...(3) And did all eat the same spiritual meat; and did all drink the same spiritual drink: for they drank of that Spiritual Rock that followed them: and that Rock was Christ," (1 Cor. 10:1-4). When our words are seasoned with God's Word, we can avoid offensive language and present them as a source of healing.

In the Hebrew Bible, ***salt*** was a crucial aspect of the sacrificial system established by Moses. Many offerings were heavily salted. Eventually, the "flavorful additive" became a symbol in divine agreements for peace. In this process of sacrificial offerings, salt was connected to the idea of permanence (durability). It became a faithful seal and a promise of peace, where there would traditionally be conflict. "For every one shall be salted with fire, and every sacrifice shall be salted with salt. Salt is good: but if the salt have lost his saltness, wherewith will ye season it? **Have salt in yourselves, and have peace one with another**," (Mrk. 9:49-50).

Present day, our unsavory and tasteless food ends up in the garbage can. Is your mouth a wellspring of praise and truth? Or a storage container for sin; filled with gossip, lies, and unsavory words? Filthy speech is selfish, often being thoughtless and a product of the flesh. The things we say reactively, out of intense emotion are impulsive. Words characterized by anger or sarcasm, that are driven by what we think and how we feel, will make us feel better in the moment, but can cause long-term pain in our relationships. Before attempting to harm others with your words, ask yourself: *Am I trying to make myself look good? Am I trying to make this other person look bad? In my desire to be funny or make a point, what do I hope to really accomplish?*

Likewise, *trash talk* can be described as insults, "throwing shade," or boastful speech. It is used to demoralize, intimidate, or humiliate someone. It is built primarily off of fear. 'Trash talk' is sinful and can corrupt the inner-man. "For they speak not peace: but they devise deceitful matters against them that are quiet in the land. Yea, they opened their mouth wide against me, and said, Aha, aha, our eye hath seen it," (Psa. 35:20-21).

Don't allow other people to make you a "garbage can" for their mess and junk. Stand firm on the principles of God in communicating with others and guard your ears. Gossip's sole purpose is to tear apart and break down the minds of the hearer. It is destructive language used to control the perception of others, and point the listener away from Christ. Think about it this way: Corrupt speech will provide no value to the hearer. It is unproductive content to fill silence, usually unimportant and untrue. This type of talk is not only foul, but allocates rottenness with us. **Often, moving fast through families, churches, and communities while wreaking havoc along the way**.

True! Even with the best of intentions, our words can come out differently than we expected or intended. The words that flow out of us indirectly reveal the "junk" or residue that is hidden in our hearts. Insecurity, hurt, unresolved anger, and pride produce words that wound. "O generation of vipers, how can ye being evil, speak good things? For out of the abundance of the heart the mouth speaketh. A good man out of the good treasure of the heart bringeth forth good things: and an evil man out of the evil treasure bringeth forth evil things," (Matt. 12:34-35).

In times like these, we must ask God to check our attitudes, soothe our discontent and heal our hearts. The human tongue uncaged can cause grief, if not tamed it can destroy. **Be mindful not to mix your poor word choice with your bad mood.** Even if you didn't mean to say it, the communication of your mouth allows the discovery of your thoughts. Those harmful words that came out of your inner-man, allowed the secrets of the heart to be made manifest. Unkind words expose unseen resentment, which must be uprooted by God.

Remember, to raise your words, and not your voice. Spiritual growth will cause us to examine ourselves, holding ourselves accountable, and encouraging us to be motivated to make verbal changes. Replace anything corrupt in your communication with the words of the Lord. Politician Pearl Strachan Hurd, is quoted saying, "Handle them carefully, for words have more power than atom bombs." Gracious speech will always point the hearer towards God. They will always nudge others to trust in and to follow Jesus.

Edifying words can implode goodness into our lives, when we speak the right things. "How is it then, brethren? When ye come together, every one of you hath a psalm, hath a doctrine, hath a tongue, hath a revelation, hath an interpretation. Let all things be done unto edifying," (1 Cor. 14:26).

While "gracious" speech is morally sound and helpful to the hearer, too often we avoid saying hard things in an effort to be "nice". We don't want to hurt feelings or strain relationships, but "nice" words are not always purposeful. "For so is the will of God, that with well doing ye may put to silence the ignorance of foolish men," (1 Pet. 2:15). The ultimate goal of gracious speech is to encourage someone to move forward in their relationship with Jesus by "ministering grace." We can speak the truth in a loving manner. We can clarify misunderstandings and offer correction through proper communication. Overall, our words should benefit, encourage, strengthen, and promote another person's spiritual well-being in love.

The supreme gift of words is a duty to be handled responsibly. Edifying speech can help someone to reach their full potential in Christ. Pursuing vocabulary that allows us to be vessels used by God, is a daily task of knowing God's Word and the wisdom to apply it. "But he answered and said, It is written, Man shall not live by bread alone, but by every word that proceedeth out of the mouth of God," (Matt. 4:4). When we eat and consume truth, it makes our own words easier to digest.

Our life becomes a perpetual ripple of what we say. A constant flow of cause and effect. When we read this, we believe that. When we think this, we say that. When we do such and such, this happens. Mother Teresa once expressed this ripple effect as an echo saying, “Kind words can be short and easy to speak, but their echoes are truly endless.” What we express in letters or words, is ultimately an attempt to articulate what is in our heart. Right words form right actions, and through the power of God they can create life-altering change.

Watch your thoughts, they become your words.

Watch your words, they become your actions.

Watch your actions, they become your habits,

Watch your habits, they become your values.

Watch your values, it becomes your destiny.

Righteous words become food for the mind and create a canvas for understanding. They flavor our world and can deliver us from trouble. “(8) O taste and see that the Lord is good: blessed is the man that trusteth in Him… (10) The young lions do lack, and suffer hunger: but they that seek the Lord shall not want any good thing,” (Psa. 34:8, 10). Depart from evil and do good today. Seek peace and pursue it. It will not happen if we are indecisive, indifferent, or passive. It takes significant effort to pursue peace and walk in Holiness. We are blessed when we take refuge in God, and allow Him to speak good things over our lives.

Grow in humility and cultivate Christ-like character by communicating effectively. While the world tells us to "Stand up for your rights!" or "Assert yourself," repeatedly encouraging us not to suffer, as a result of verbal abuse. God's Word on the contrary says, if someone insults you do not return the disrespect, but instead say or do something kind. "Woe unto you that are full! For ye shall hunger. Woe unto you that laugh now! For ye shall mourn and weep. Woe unto you, when all men shall speak well of you! For so did their fathers to false prophets. But I say unto you which hear, Love your enemies, do good to them which hate you, bless them that curse you, and pray for them which despitefully use you," (Lk. 6:25-28).

Healthy relationships are based off of good communication. We must practice and apply God's principles in our everyday lives. We must crave and desire to speak and walk in love. Self-seeking behavior builds barriers in our conversation, causing many to demand their own way. These selfish hindrances cause us to speak and listen in disregard for God and others. We all have different backgrounds, personalities, and ways of thinking. Through reconciliation and a petition for change, we can absorb offense and mend strained relationships. God's Word is a sure guide to reconcile our lives back to Him. "Let nothing be done through strife or vainglory; but in lowliness of mind let each esteem other better than themselves," (Phil. 2:3).

Seasoned speech is harmonious. Having a high regard for oneself will prevent an individual from admitting their wrongs, and cause them to get angry when their way is challenged. Rejecting correction, and venting is not a fruit of the spirit. "Let us therefore follow after the things which make for peace, and things wherewith one may edify another. For meat destroy not the work of God. All things indeed are pure; but it is evil for that man who eateth with offence," (Rom. 14:19-20).

Through humility, we can learn of God and learn of others. Do not be deceived by wrong words, but be open to hearing what others have to say. While deception is a snare, the truth of God is always right. Deceiving words and actions are typically calculated. In an attempt to manipulate, deceive, mislead and distort the facts it becomes sinful communication. This skewed view of reality can cause exaggeration, and lead to deliberate use of phrases such as 'You always,' or 'You never.' We must work diligently to speak truthfully, relying on the scriptures to lead us in what to say.

In our friendships, work-relationships, marriages, and communication within ministry, we must be mindful not to trade insults or make accusations. Truth without love can be insensitive, harsh, and cruel. As believers, we have not been appointed to wrath but to obtain salvation. We must watch and being sober, comforting and edifying one another through the Word. If we have one mind, which is the mind of Christ, then we should all be speaking the same thing. "Now we exhort you, brethren, warn them that are unruly, comfort the feebleminded, support the weak, be patient towards all men. See that none render evil for evil unto any man; but ever follow that which is good, both among yourselves, and to all men," (1 Thess. 5:14-15).

When someone mistreats you, giving them the silent treatment is not reflective of how God want us to respond. Godly communication requires that we turn from evil words and are honest in our body language, mannerisms, and intent. Be sure to bless others with speech that builds up, giving thanks in all things. The Word of God should go before us and direct us in every area of our lives.

> *"And thou shalt love the Lord thy God with all thine heart, and with all thy soul, and with all thy might.* ***And these words****, which I command thee this day, shall be in thine heart: And thou shalt teach them diligently unto thy children, and shalt talk of them when thou sittest in thine house, and when thou walkest by the way, and when thou liest down, and when thou riseth up. And thou shalt bind them for a sign upon thine hand, and they shall be as frontlets between thine eyes. And thou shalt write them upon the posts of thy house, and on thy gates,"* (Deut. 6:5-9).

Every day is another opportunity for the Holy Spirit to mature us, no matter our age, the place that we find ourselves in, or the circumstances we need to Him to 'breathe' into. In the faith, our senses are constantly being exercised and developed, being seasoned and processed, to discern both good and evil. We must constantly listen, learn, and live in truth - going on to *perfection* (Eph. 4:25-26).

Continue to regard God for being a way-maker, a miracle-worker, a promise-keeper, and a light in dark places. Our respect and honor for His Word, causes us to be an example of His goodness with our words. Allow God to flavor your life and give you freedom today. Allow God to color your words to represent His character. "Neither have I gone back from the commandment of His lips; I have esteemed the words of His mouth more than my necessary food," (Job 23:12).

God desires for all of His people to speak with changed hearts. In order to speak without flaw, on this side of Heaven, it requires sufficient spiritual inventory and discipline. Allow your words to bake in truth, being seared with righteousness, and handled for other's consumption. We must recall the scriptures daily in order to communicate, function, and relate with others as Christ. "Doth not the ear try words? And the mouth taste His meat?" (Job 12:11). After tasting the good Word of God, we are no longer dull of hearing, but open and fully responsible for everything that we utter in His name. Seasoned speech is not developed overnight, but through a mind saturated with the Word of God. Through Christ's example, we can all strive to be full of His Spirit, as well as full of His words.

SCRIPTURE SUMMARY

Deuteronomy 6:5-9

Job 12:11

Job 23:12

Psalms 12:2-4

Psalms 34:8, 10

Psalms 35:20-21

Psalms 139:4

Psalms 140:1-3

Proverbs 10:21, 32

Proverbs 25:11

Matthew 4:4

Matthew 12:34-25

Mark 9:49-50

Romans 2:4

Romans 14:19-20

1 Corinthians 10:1-4

1 Corinthians 14:26

2 Corinthians 2:15

Ephesians 4:25-26

Philippians 2:3

Colossians 4:6

1 Thessalonians 5:14-15

1 Peter 2:15

CHECK YOUR UNDERSTANDING

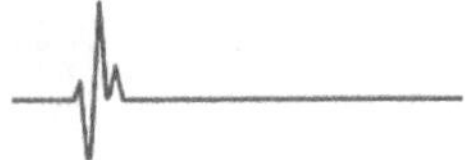

1. A word fitly spoken is like apples of gold in pictures of silver (Proverbs 25:11).

   (True) **(False)**

2. Raise your words, not your ____________.

3. What scripture says, "with our tongue we will prevail; our lips are our own: who is Lord over us?"

   (a) Psalms 12:4

   (b) Psalms 12:2

   (c) Proverbs 10:32

4. Purity of speech reflects purity of ____________.

5. What scripture says, "Set a watch, O Lord, before my mouth; keep the door of my lips?"

   (a) 2 Corinthians 2:15

   (b) Psalms 141:3

   (c) Mark 9:49-50

6. 'Trash talk' is insulting or boastful speech that is used to demoralize, intimidate, or humiliate someone.

   (True) **(False)**

6 HEART CHECK

What we articulate out of our mouth is a direct reflection of how we feel in our hearts. Truthfully, we should color our worlds an imaginary shade of "red" because our actions, emotions, words, perspective, and relationships are all derived from the tiny heart organ that beats in our chest. *Ba-dom! Ba-dom!* As this sound gives life, and beats on the inside of the body, an assortment of words stemming from its condition develop on the outside. The heart has the potential to bless or curse, corrupt or condemn, give courage or create fear, build barriers or fix our thinking, even destroy and change lives.

Our heart often seeks to create an authentic narrative, but without disciplined words the translation suffers. We all want to communicate how we feel, what we desire, where we want to go, and what we need. However, without a transformed heart, a renewed mind, and Godly speech our words are often misquoted, misunderstood, and unpursued.

Traveling in the air, landing on deaf ears. Sent out, and received with no purpose or change as a result.

According to a 2020 motivational business article, "99% of the harm in our lives is initiated in our own head, by our own thoughts. 1% of the harm is caused by reality, what actually happens and the outcome. **Most of the time, the problem isn't the problem.** The way we think, how we feel, and what we say about the problem is." Saying how you feel can empower you, releasing you from an emotional hold, and allowing you to confront the trauma in your life. Nonetheless, when your words align with God's Word, you become positioned for real success. "Offer the sacrifices of righteousness, and put your trust in the Lord," (Psa. 4:5).

Jesus came with all-power to bring total deliverance on the Earth. That means that *you*, *I*, *he*, *she*, or *them* being unshackled from the clutches of sin and despair. An individual free from fornication and sexual sin, but addicted to drugs has won half of the battle. Or another, being free from old criminal habits and theft, but having a bad mind just won't do. Or even, being free from anger or rage, but struggling with gossip and backbiting isn't full-circle. "For whosoever shall keep the whole law, and yet offend in one point, he is guilty of all," (Jam. 2:10). God loves us so much that He wants to help, heal, and direct our words and actions in a new and endearing way. He wants to transform our lives completely, so that we are perfect and complete in Him.

If you want to check your heart, listen to your words. Some of us are too embarrassed to accept our own reality, unwilling to acknowledge the truth. While, walking in your authenticity may cause earthquakes in other people's fairytales, don't suppress it. Let the Holy Spirit have its way. Unhealed trauma can look like being sensitive to conflict or feeling frustrated when you are not in control. Remember that Earth has no sorrow, that Heaven cannot heal.

Let God into your heart today! Give Him room to settle, rebuild, rearrange, and restore. Our desire should be to hear what is being said without the filter of old wounds. We must surrender our lives and our words to God. "Who is a wise man and endued with knowledge among you? Let him shew out of a good conversation his works with meekness of wisdom. But if ye have bitter envying and strife in your hearts, glory not, and lie not against the truth. The wisdom that descendeth not from above, but is earthly, sensual, devilish. For where envying and strife is, there is confusion and every evil work," (Jam. 3:13-16).

Our responsibility, as believers, is to work together and to love others. Always choose to speak from a healed place, and if you are still healing ask God to direct your words so that you do not harm others. Don't be the pebble that causes a flood of negativity in someone else's life. If you allow your words spill out of a sin-filled heart, you'll drown in regret later. "The heart of the righteous studieth to answer: but the mouth of the wicked poureth out evil things," (Prov. 15:28). Christ has created us for more and redeemed us for greater. As the Sons and/or Daughters of God, we should be blameless and harmless, without rebuke, amongst a crooked and perverse nation. In times like these, every believer must work out their own salvation with fear and trembling (Phil. 2:12). Seek God!

Instead of negative talk, switch gears by thinking about the consequences of such dialogue first. A circulated quote says, "Before you argue with someone, ask yourself: Is this person mentally mature enough to grasp the concept of a different perspective? If not, there is no point to argue." Instead, replace your discontent and attention by focusing on the things of God. *What are you trying to accomplish by saying that? Is that really the best course of action?* Then, ask yourself: *Is this the right time to mention this? Is this spiritually edifying to say?* "A good man out of the good treasure of his heart bringeth forth that which is good; and an evil man out of the evil treasure of his heart bringeth forth that which is evil: for out of the abundance of the heart his mouth speaketh," (Lk. 6:45).

Walking in the Spirit of God, makes no provision for the flesh. Every person is fighting a hard battle and holding an untold story. Some souls choose to endure silently, to suffer in the shadows, choosing to seek God alone through trials and tribulation. We often hear: *Did you hear what "such and such" did? Oh, child! Did you hear what "such and such" said?* It's never the rumor that hurts, but often the audacity of 'the mouth' it came from. **If your family member, friend, leader, co-worker, or neighbor *really* told you their life story... you'd apologize for what you thought, said,**

and spread about them based on what you assumed or heard. Backbiting and gossip, murmuring and complaining, hate-filled speech and presumptuous actions will eventually destroy lives. "Neither murmur ye, as some of them also murmured, and were destroyed of the destroyer," (1 Cor. 10:10).

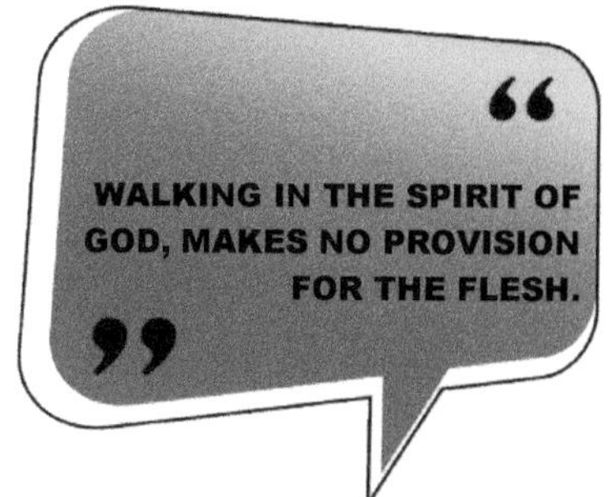

Listen to others with an open mind, but be careful what you receive in your heart. Criticism may come from someone you would not accept advice from. "Let not then your good be evil spoken of," (Rom. 14:16). While we cannot waste precious time chasing lies, hiding from the truth, defending our own reputations, or engaging against every "growl" (so to speak), we can adjust our associations and increase our prayer life. Position yourself with those committed to spiritual growth, those who are trying to make positive changes. Evil communication *can* corrupt your good manners (1 Cor. 15:33). Be mindful to seek wise counsel in all things, and remember that God's Word always has the final say concerning you and your family.

Sometimes, we make strides towards those who mean us no good. *Stand still* and allow God to direct your associations, relationships, and your words the right way. Focus your heart and attention on Him. "And ye shall seek me, and find me, when ye shall search for me with all your heart," (Jer. 29:13). Try to avoid actions that might encourage others to violate their own conscience by abstaining from even the appearance of evil. Be blameless in your talk, and faithful to the call and work set before you (1 Thess. 5:22-24). Rejoice evermore and give thanks in all things! Be kind to yourself and be kind to others!

REVERENCING LEADERSHIP

The condition of your heart can affect the way that you serve. While there are many who love God and are found faithful, there are also many who go astray. An individual can leave God's presence when they find pleasure in lies. By tottering this metaphorical "spiritual fence," they may bless others with their mouths, but curse God inwardly (Psa. 62:2-4). No matter the circumstance or difficulties that we may find ourselves in, a mature believer will never curse God, curse their crisis, or speak negatively about their pastors or leadership.

Having a servant's heart, is to have a mindset and a desire to serve others selflessly and sacrificially. Regardless of your feelings towards people or what others may have said, a true servant doesn't look to his own interests, but holds others in high regard, especially leadership. A true servant committed to serving others. These type of leaders are aligned with God's Spirit and embrace humility. They are focused on growth, they value people, and understand that there is no honor among gossip.

Gossip or "*whispering*" plants seeds of doubt and mistrust in the heart of others, allowing rebellion to take root. God has entrusted the spiritual well-being of an entire congregation to who He has called for a specific purpose. Gossiping about them just increases their burden. Examine yourself and pray for your church leadership instead. Negative support and conflict, undermines the good work that God is doing in and through the local ministry. "Saying, touch not mine anointed, and do my prophets no harm," (Psa. 105:15).

Those who represent Christ well will guard themselves against divisive discussions (Rom. 16:17). "For which things' sake the wrath of God cometh on the children of disobedience: In the which ye also walked sometime, when ye lived in them. But now you also put off all these: anger, wrath, malice, blasphemy, filthy communication out of your mouth, lie not one to another, seeing that ye have put off the old man with his deeds; and have put on the new man, which is renewed in knowledge after the image of Him that created him," (Col. 3:6-10).

Our natural tendency is to share "news," but before we share information that is not ours, we must first ask: *Is this information loving or constructive? Is the person I am sharing this with part of the solution? Have I talked to my pastor first before I talk about him/her?* When you approach matters directly rather than behind gossip and slander, you can stop damaging rumors, and prove yourself trustworthy to those of spiritual authority. If we cannot answer these questions in God-honoring ways, it is best to keep the information to ourselves (Jam. 3:5-6). We must all come together in the unity of the faith, to speak the truth in love, and grow in the knowledge of God (Eph. 4:11-15).

***Excerpts/ References from "Church answers" article*

In difficult situations, the contents of our hearts are revealed. When you continue to have a positive attitude even when life is testing you, it will ultimately synchronize your heart to the rhythm of God's heart. Faith allows you to operate in His Spirit. "A soft answer turneth away wrath, but grievous words stir up anger," (Prov. 15:1). Have you ever said something contrary to what was expected, and someone responded with, "There is something different about you?" *If you want to be trusted, be honest.* Sometimes, the truth of our everyday situations is hidden in immense pain, discarded under sin, condensed in our words, and unable to be described verbally. If our emotions are contained, God cannot hear our prayers. Be authentic and allow the Holy Ghost to work in you. Biblical truth is available, open and transparent to all, but we must seek after it and ultimately desire to be better.

In all things, we can find comfort and consolation through Christ. **It *is* possible to be capable and lost, smiling and struggling, kind and have boundaries, loving and questioning, successful and traumatized, valuable and flawed, vulnerable and powerful.** Asking: *Don't you care God? Don't* *you see that I am hurting? Don't you hear my thoughts? Don't you hear circulating and evil words in others?* In moments when the noise of the world seems louder than the truth, cling to the God that never changes. There is no Earthly place we can hide in, that the Lord is not there (Psa. 139:7-8). He see's and He knows.

Through salvation, our hearts are made new. Our speech is guiding light to those who sit in darkness. Who will help the lost? Who will emerge against evil? Who will stand up against the workers of iniquity and speak the Word of God boldly? *You can!* Someone needs to hear your heart. Someone needs to hear your testimony. Your words can bring about deliverance. In Holiness, we can speak the truth without fear, in order to draw others towards Christ. "But judgment shall return unto righteousness: and all the upright in heart shall follow it," (Psa. 94:15). We can all encourage righteousness, once our own obedience towards God has been fulfilled (2 Cor. 10:5-6).

Ultimately, communication is about content and delivery, fifty-fifty. What you say matters, but how you say it, and how you relate with folks, is what differentiates righteous words from condemning talk. Through truth, a merciful tongue can help those who are lost find their way. Ultimately, it is God's Word that pricks hearts and shifts conversations. Speech derived from a clean heart and pure hands opens ears and causes change. **Our desire as servants should be to lead with compassion.** "Who shall ascend into the hill of the Lord? Or who shall stand in His Holy place?

He that hath clean hands, and a pure heart; who hath not lifted His soul unto vanity, nor sworn deceitfully," (Psa. 24:3-4).

A kind heart begets a kind word. *Kindness* is defined as the quality of being friendly, generous, and considerate; being charitable to help. It is also associated with altruism, affection, benevolence, courtesy, decency, forbearance, gentleness, and cordiality. "But the fruit of the Spirit is love, joy, peace, longsuffering, gentleness, goodness, faith, meekness, temperance: against such there is no law," (Gal. 5:22-23). According to a benevolence and psychology article, practicing kindness can cause positive mental and physical changes, lowering stress and anxiety, reducing blood pressure, and boosting the immune system. You show compassion by being there to listen, focusing on others, offering a helping hand, staying connected, expecting good things to happen, even smiling and complimenting others. A moment of support for someone in a time of need, even a quiet word of encouragement, can make a world of difference to someone.

> "THE MOUTH WILL SPEAK WHAT THE HEART IS FULL OF."

<u>**Principles of Kindness**</u> *(gentleness):*

- We must be aware of the opportunity to be kind
- We must be prepared to suspend judgment, leaving the situation to a higher power and authority

- Through action, we must show kindness by being friendly and considerate to the person available to us (Prov. 18:24).
- We must offer kindness without conditions, or expectations of recognition and reward

Discipling our words is a process. *Yes!* Indifference and cruelty exist in the world today, but as believers we can choose to follow Christ in how we communicate. Of course, there will be a difference of opinions, conflicting ideas, and difficult conversations at work, at home, at school, and in ministry. Yet, we are responsible for being an example of kindness. That "joke" you said may be the only thing that someone remembers about a business, an event, or a person. What you said in a moment of anger could be the last straw or breaking point, for somebody who is desperately trying to make it through a difficult week. The effects of dangerous and deadly conversations can happen in an instant, but are often irreversible. "A merry heart maketh a cheerful countenance: but by sorrow of the heart the spirit is broken," (Prov. 15:13).

Speak with caution. The mouth will speak what the heart is full of. Your words have influence, hearken to the voice of God for instruction. Listen and obey His commandments. Then, be careful of what you speak, also being mindful of what you listen to. **Then, stop letting other people speak their fears into God's plans.** Close your ears to negative opinions that oppose God's instruction. "My voice shalt thou hear in the morning, O Lord; in the morning will I direct my prayer unto thee, and look up," (Psa.

5:3). Constant learners will write up their plans in pencil, then give God the eraser and a pen. God can create good in our lives, better than we could have ever hoped or imagined.

What are you creating with your words? A sharp tongue, envy, and pride put us at odds with God, but prayer and humility endears us to Him. You can be up today, and down tomorrow. Therefore, be humble with your words and kind with your actions. "Boast not thyself of to morrow; for thou knowest not what a day may bring forth. Let another man praise thee, and not thine own mouth; a stranger, and not thine own lips," (Prov. 27:1-2). Turn to the Bible in times of distress. Turn to the Bible when you need direction on what to do, or what to say. God will not despise a broken and a contrite heart (Psa. 51:17). When we invite His presence into our lives, we honor Him with our lips.

Healthy spirituality depends on having a harmonious relationship with the Holy Spirit. Your health is your wealth. Make your heart the most attractive quality about you. "Thy Word have I hid in mine heart, that I might not sin against thee," (Psa. 119:11). When something you *say* does not "sit well" with your spirit, it should convict you. Your thoughts will either accuse or excuse you (Rom. 2:15). Possessing the mind of Christ and the heart of God, causes believers in Christ to speak and interact with others differently. **Purity of heart sets a standard, conforming our character after Christ.** Our outer world, and what is going on around us is a direct reflection of our inner world. May the Lord grant you the courage and clarity to communicate your needs, hopes, and desires in this season. *Change your talk, to change your walk with God!* When you approach each moment with fresh eyes and an open heart, you are no longer defined by your past pain or your fears for the future. "Keep thy heart with all diligence; for out of it are the issues of life," (Prov. 4:23).

Joy is not found in our ever-changing circumstances. Keep walking in purpose and serving the Lord with gladness, despite what may be going on around you. Real joy cannot be found in a person, a profession, or material possessions – it must be found in God. We can endure discriminatory treatment, evil words spoken, and difficult people because the Lord's coming is sure. Not only is He is Lord of the *possible*, but also the *impossible*. Not only, is He is Lord over *kind* people, but also *difficult* people. Continue to seek God.

Ba-dom! Ba-dom! The greatest tragedy is not untimely death, but inadvertently a life that is void of God. Is your heartbeat in tune with the Spirit? Do you speak from a position of charity and love? In Him, we can speak positive words daily and have hope. Now is the time more than ever to pursue Jesus. Our faith gives us patience, and our patience strengthens our faith. "A new heart also will I give you, and a new spirit will I put within you: and I will take away the stony heart out of your flesh, and I will give you an heart of flesh," (Eze. 36:26). **Ask God to give you brand new words to speak, a new mindset, a new outlook, some new hope, and a new spirit today.** *With God, all things are possible.*

SCRIPTURE SUMMARY

Psalms 4:5
Psalms 5:3
Psalms 24:3-4
Psalms 51:17
Psalms 62:2-4
Psalms 94:15
Psalms 105:15
Psalms 119:11
Psalms 139:7-8
Proverbs 4:23
Proverbs 15:1
Proverbs 15:13
Proverbs 15:28
Proverbs 18:24
Proverbs 27:1-2
Jeremiah 29:13
Ezekiel 36:26
Luke 6:45
Romans 2:15
Romans 4:16
Romans 16:17
1 Corinthians 10:10
1 Corinthians 15:33
2 Corinthians 10:5-6
Galatians 5:22-23
Ephesians 4:11-15
Philippians 2:12
Colossians 3:6-10

SCRIPTURE SUMMARY

1 Thessalonians 5:22-24

James 2:10

James 3:13-16

CHECK YOUR UNDERSTANDING

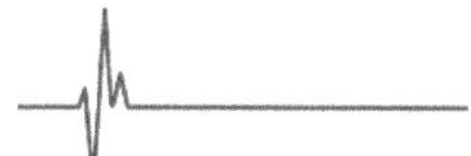

Down:

1. The condition of your heart can affect the way that you...
2. Walking in the spirit of God makes no provision for the ____.
4. Psalms 4:5 says to offer the sacrifices of righteousness, and put your ______ in the Lord.
6. This scripture mentions working our your own salvation with ___ and trembling (Phil. 2:12)

Across:

3. What we articulate out of our mouth is a direct reflection of how we feel in our....
5. For where envying and ____ is, there is confusion and every evil work (Jam. 3:16)
7. Offending in one point of the whole law, means we are guilty of ____ (Jam. 2:10)

7 GOOD NEWS

Have you ever read a newspaper article, watched the news, overheard a conversation, or got a phone call that made you smile? Uplifting news can give you goosebumps, an unexpected burst of positivity that you want to share with everyone and everything. In Christianity, the gospel, or *good news* is the widely shared broadcast or bulletin of the imminent coming of the Kingdom of God. It is the greatest and most prolific story ever told. "...The time is fulfilled, and the Kingdom of God is at hand: repent ye, and believe the gospel," (Mrk. 1:15).

The Bible's purpose is to reconcile man back to God. In our humanity, it inspires people by giving them an opportunity to find salvation. Being loved by God, renewed in our mind, and saved from the blazes of hell is *good news*! Being called apart, separated from the world, delivered from sin, and able to overcome life's obstacles is *good news*! The "good book" is a beacon of hope, to be cherished and shared by every believer. In our wretched state, it has been a pathway towards redemption and freedom. Deliverance can be the destiny of everyone who calls on the name of Jesus!

We ignite change by sharing this good news and connecting with people from all around the world. “Having then gifts differing according to the grace that is given to us, whether prophecy, let us prophecy according to the proportion of faith; or ministry, let us wait on our ministering: or he that teacheth, on teaching; or he that exhorteth, on exhortation: he that giveth, let him do it with simplicity; he that ruleth, with diligence; he that sheweth mercy, with cheerfulness,” (Rom. 12:6-8).. The universe responds to the spoken Word of God.

Your beliefs fuel the power of God inside you, activating possibility, and perseverance, and purpose. **A lack of faith affects how you serve, how you give, how you talk, and what you believe**. You must believe that the goodness of God will always defeat and overcome evil. “Be not overcome of evil, but overcome evil with good,” (Rom. 12:21). *There are no coincidences. We create what we speak.* Prayer works. Through meditation, our inner-man can attract great things. Connect with God in the ordinary, extraordinary, and everyday moments of life. There is no getting out of bed, without God. There is no making breakfast, without God. There is no driving to work, without God. There is no problem solving, without God. There is no riding your bike, without God. There is no wealth, without God. There is no victory, without God (Jn. 15:5). He upholds the universe by the Words of His power, and hearing and obeying His voice allows us to be an imprint of His nature. “For in Him we live, move, and have our being; as certain also of your own poets have said, For we are His offspring," (Acts 17:28). **So, let us not build for the moment, but for eternity.**

Be encouraged! You can be fruitful in the midst of your frustration. Be sure that your lips and your life are preaching the same thing. Be sure that the messages from your mouth and your heart coincide. You will be tested by major changes, delayed promises, unanswered prayers, undeserved criticism, senseless tragedies, but know that all things work together for the good of those who love the Lord, and are called according to His purpose (Rom. 8:28).

The word "no" is negative but the word "knowing" is positive. In Him, there isn't a "nay" or "no," His Word says that we *can* do all things through Christ who strengthens us. Moreover, the word *"know"* is defined as sensing, recognizing, understanding, appreciating, or realizing through observation. It is an inquiry, or receiving of information, that there is more than meets the eye. As believers, we *know* that everything negative in our lives, will in due course be purposed to benefit us. At some point, life works out for our good. It is our job to wait in faith, following God, and watching our words while we wait. "Seek ye the Lord while He may be found, call upon Him while He is near," (Isa. 55:6).

Trust in the Word of God! It never betrays, it will never let you down. "In the beginning was the Word, and the Word was with God, and the Word was God," (Jn. 1:1). Challenges will come, but having the mind of Christ will allow you to speak to your circumstances. You can defy the odds. God gave you a fingerprint that no one else has, so that you can leave an imprint no one else can. In spite of every shortcoming, every season of lack, every failure, every flaw, every insecurity, God has the power to renew us from deep within and cause us to rise from the ashes, better than before. Not through our effort or natural sense, but through His transforming grace and supernatural power.

> "LET US NOT BUILD FOR THE MOMENT, BUT FOR ETERNITY."

The good news is that in your quirkiness and misfit ways, you can change the world. God has already conquered fear, death, and defeat so that you don't have to. If you need to slay some giants in your life, if you need deliverance, if you need a promotion or a financial breakthrough, say: *I've got this!* "Through God we shall do valiantly: for He it is that shall tread down our enemies," (Psa. 108:13). Through affliction, heaviness of heart, persecution, and misunderstandings you must continue to press forward towards the mark, which is Christ Jesus. In order to truly grasp the magnitude of what God wants to do in your life, you must first understand His Word. "Trust in the Lord with all thine heart; and *lean not* unto thine own understanding. In all thy ways acknowledge Him, and He shall direct thy path," (Prov. 3:5-6).

There is a specific sound, set and ringing, across this great and terrible nation. The *good news* is the sound of the trumpet is blasting, but are you listening? "Cry aloud, spare not, lift up thy voice like a trumpet, and shew my people their transgressions, and the House of Jacob their sins," (Isa. 58:1). Remember, you are more than a conqueror through Christ. Do not use your mouth to speak evil of others, in doing this you hinder your own blessings. Do not yield your members to harm others, becoming an instrument of sin or unrighteousness. God has given you authority to do good to those who mean you harm. He has given you the authority to dominate in these wayward days of destruction. You can rule in the midst of your enemies (Psa. 110:2). You can love in the midst of hate. You can speak God's Word in the middle of controversy.

God is calling you to be new, clean, Holy, and sanctified in Him. He has chosen you, delivered you, and filled you to the brim with His Spirit, for such a times as this. You can make a difference in the lives of others. "But ye are a chosen generation, a royal priesthood, a Holy nation, a peculiar people; that ye should shew forth the praises of Him who hath called you out of darkness into His marvellous light," (1 Pet. 2:9). May you refuse to connect the dots based on your painful experiences and draw the wrong conclusions about yourself and about God. May you refuse to be a product of your past. May you allow God's love to define, refine, and teach you. May you insist on living as one who has a redemptive story to tell (Heb. 12:2).

Do not faint or be wearied in your minds. You can do exceedingly and abundantly above all that you ask of think, according to His Holy power working down on the inside of you (Eph. 3:20). God is the author and finisher of your faith. He formed you in your mother's womb and is aware of your desires, shortcomings, and needs. The *good news* is that if we ask anything according to His will, He will hear us (1 Jn. 5:14). God quickened us when we were dead in our sins, and made us alive again. We are His workmanship, created in Christ Jesus for good works. In this new state, we no longer walk according to the conversation of times past, according to the course of the world, but through faith He has made us part of a covenant of promise (Eph. 2:2-10).

What does God want to show you today? *Will you listen to Him speak?* When we put God first, everything else falls into its proper place or either drops out of our lives. **The love of the Lord will govern the claims for our affection, the demands for our time, the interests we pursue, and the order of our priorities.** We must be willing, ready, inclined, prepared, able, and predisposed for His Spirit to reign in us. We are not righteous in God's eyes because of commitment, good works, His piety, our intellect, or anything else other than Him choosing us before the foundations of the world. Let us continuously acknowledge the sovereignty and authority of God. Public speaker, Michael Altshuler is quoted saying, "The bad news is time flies. The good news is you're the pilot." Tomorrow is not promised to any of us, only God remains our hope in these last days.

We must discern the signs of the times. God is on His way back and we must continue to choose Christ, follow leadership, and serve Him wholeheartedly (Josh. 24:15). If we are Abraham's children, we should do the works of Abraham. "I know that ye are Abraham's seed; but ye seek to kill me, because my Word hath no place in you," (Jn. 8:37). Put truth in your heart today. We are a people under God's authority. A royal priesthood, a chosen generation with dominion and power, precedence and favor, able to put all things under our feet.

> **"WHEN WE FRAME OUR WORDS TO KNIT TOGETHER AND NOT TEAR APART, WE MAKE EACH OTHER"**

While the times may change, and laws may change, and pandemics may exist, and the world may struggle to understand *what is next*? God's Word is stable. It is the ultimate source for answers. He is the same, yesterday, today, and forever. "For verily I say unto you, till Heaven and Earth pass, one jot or tittle shall in no wise pass from the law, till all be fulfilled," (Matt. 5:18). Everything you need for life, happiness, and Godliness can be found in the book. You must put His Word inside of you to manifest miracles outside of you! Pray bold prayers. Use your mouth to speak life and not death. There is power in what you believe, what you think, and what you say. Use your words for good, to build and to bring hope.

We were all created with purpose in mind. *Purpose* is defined as the reason something is done or created; the motivation, cause, reason, occasion, intention, objective, usefulness, or benefit for which something exists. It is the reason we get up in the morning to pray, to praise, to care for our families, to give a kind word to others, or to pursue our daily assignment, tasks and jobs. Whether you are bringing souls in, or bringing in finances, or helping leadership, or praising during worship, or on the cameras, or an usher greeting members as they come in, or helping administratively, or doing Kingdom-business, or cleaning the bathrooms. Whatever your specific purpose may be, do it with all of your might, serving the Lord with gladness.

God is always able to make grace abound toward you, that you may have sufficiency to every good work. Be committed to the vision of the House and the vision of your leaders. “To everything there is a season, and a time to every purpose under the Heaven,” (Ecc. 3:1). God does not forget your work and labour of love that you have shown towards His House and His people. He will reward you for your faithfulness. He knows every seed that you have sown, every time you have sacrificed your time for the greater good. Also, every time you imparted your gift for the exaltation of God’s Word, and every time you have given a child a cup of water. “Thou hast proved mine heart; thou hast visited me in the night; thou hast tried me, and shalt find nothing; I am purposed that my mouth shall not transgress,” (Psa. 17:3).

We are able to speak positive words, and work together by being mission-conscious. We make ourselves better through maximizing each other's strengths and building on each other's weaknesses. When we frame our words to knit together and not tear apart, we make each other better. When your heart is pure and your intentions are for good, no good thing will He withhold from you when you walk upright before Him. "Every purpose is established by counsel and with good advice make war," (Prov. 20:18). We are living in the last days. It is so important to set our hearts and our affections on the right things. "The Lord of hosts hath sworn, saying, surely as I have thought, so shall it come to pass; and as I have purposed, so shall it stand," (Isa. 14:24).

Continue to work, build, love, give, pray, worship, and serve. Allow yourself to be an instrument used by the Creator for good. In order to be a vessel used for His glory, you must be willing to surrender and serve with a grateful heart. When God established the foundations of the Earth, He formed you in your mother's womb for a reason and with a plan in mind.

As we walk with God, we must love Him deep. True love requires you to give up those things which have weighed you down – sin is heavy. In order to live in the fullness of God, we must be free from backbiting, negative thinking, addiction, deceit, lies, lust, and any sin that can cause a breach between us and God. As for our iniquities, we have known of them, they have testified against us, but it is His Spirit which brings full deliverance. “Righteousness shall go before Him; and shall set us in the way of His steps,” (Psa. 85:13).

Despair drains our faith and runs deep. We must trash negative thoughts and treasure our experiences. His love will always triumph over the power of sin. Put on the garment of praise for the spirit of heaviness and proclaim this as the battle of the Lord. “To appoint unto them that mourn in Zion, to give unto them beauty for ashes, the oil of joy for mourning, the garment of praise for the spirit of heaviness; that they might be called trees of righteousness, the planting of the Lord, that He might be glorified,” (Isa. 61:3).

Learning to be calm when you are disrespected, hurt, or angry is a force of faith which exemplifies supernatural power. **Your mind is a magnet. If you think of blessings, you'll attract blessings. If you think of problems, you'll attract problems.** Always cultivate good thoughts and remain positive. “My little children, let us not love in word, neither in tongue, but in deed and in truth,” (1 Jn. 3:18). We must speak from a place of peace, not based on our frustrations or how we may feel.

In Matthew chapter five, it compels us to love God with everything in us, from the depths of our soul we acknowledge and praise Him. Blessed are the poor in spirit: for theirs is the Kingdom of Heaven. Blessed are they that mourn, for they shall be comforted. Blessed are the meek, for they shall inherit the Earth. Blessed are they which do hunger and thirst after righteousness: for they shall be filled. Blessed are the merciful, for they shall obtain mercy. Blessed are the pure in heart: for they shall see God. Blessed are the peacemakers: for they shall be called the children of God. Rejoice, and be exceeding glad knowing that there is a great reward in Heaven for your suffering, for every tear, and for every trial that you go through.

Your miracle is in your mouth! It belongs to you. The scriptures have supernatural capability, but do we really understand the depths of God's voice? Can we fathom the control in His commands, or the power the law truly contains? As believers, do we even know how to activate it? In the beginning of creation, God's Spirit moved upon the face of the waters, and He spoke. All He had to say was: *"Let there be,"* (Gen. 1:2-3). You have to stop speaking to the leaves and branches of your situation, and speak to the root of that "thing." Your prayers are bouncing off of walls because you have not given God back His Word. *You have to say it!*

The good news is that His Word is immutable. That means, it is unchanging, unalterable, absolute, and undeniable (Num. 23:19, Heb. 6:18). So, when the Bible says, speak the Word only and my servant shall be healed, you can believe it (Matt. 8:8). When it says, all things are possible to those that believe, you can stand on it (Mk. 9:23). When He says, I've put every one of your tears in a bottle, assuring you that they are in His book. Know that He understands your struggles and setbacks (Psa. 56:8). When He says, a liberal soul shall be made fat, you can rely on it

(Prov. 11:25). When He says, no weapon that is formed against you shall prosper and every tongue that shall rise up in judgment, He will condemn, you can trust Him in battle (Isa. 54:17).

I cannot tell you how long you are going to go through what you are going through, but I can tell you that you are going to make it (1 Pet. 4:12-13). The voice of God will never contradict the Word of God. In repentance and quietness, God shows His strength. Underneath His everlasting arms there is peace and safety. Our world is hurt and broken. Even so, we know that whatever we may face, that the Lord is a very present help in times of need. Everything that He does is just, appointed, good, and right. "For whatsoever things were written aforetime were written for our learning, that we through patience and comfort of the scriptures might have hope," (Rom. 15:4).

"YOUR MIRACLE IS IN YOUR MOUTH."

We must constantly look to God, and be in expectation of what His Word says, being conscious of what He is able to do. For the diagnosis that you didn't see coming, for the child that walked away, for the pain pulsing through your body, for the relationship that is growing apart, for the time you spent in recovery, for the loved one you lost, for the aches of loneliness you feel as you sit in silence, remember that God is able! Don't give up and don't give in! Pray, even when you can't figure it out. Pray, even when it doesn't make sense. Pray, even when things look impossible. *God is able!*

Do you know who holds tomorrow? What are you trusting Him for today? Every day is a gift. So, we must always give Him glory! The time is now to repent, to release, to go deeper in His Word, and to make God our everything. The Lord has given you everything you need to succeed, but you will need to step up, stand still, and speak differently. Be prepared for spiritual change. The Heavens are open, but we must prepare our minds and hearts to encounter the Lord.

In Christ, we find purpose for the pain, strength for the struggle, and faith for the fight (1 Tim. 6:12). When the Holy Spirit fills our life, it causes us to get better spiritually, to be better physically, and to feel better emotionally. Everything that we need can be found in the scriptures. The *good news* is that we can tap into this supernatural power daily, when we choose to *say it, speak it...and believe.*

SCRIPTURE SUMMARY

Genesis 1:2-3

Numbers 23:19

Joshua 24:15

Psalms 17:3

Psalms 56:8

Psalms 85:13

Psalms 108:13

Psalms 110:2

Proverbs 3:5-6

Proverbs 11:25

Proverbs 20:18

Ecclesiastes 3:1

Isaiah 14:24

Isaiah 54:17

Isaiah 55:6

Isaiah 58:1

Isaiah 61:3

Matthew 5:18

Matthew 8:8

Mark 1:15

Mark 9:23

John 1:1

John 8:37

John 15:5

Acts 17:28

Romans 8:28

Romans 12:6-8, 21

Romans 15:4

SCRIPTURE SUMMARY

Ephesians 2:2-10

Ephesians 3:20

1 Timothy 6:12

Hebrews 6:18

Hebrews 12:2

1 Peter 2:9

1 Peter 4:12-13

1 John 3:18

CHECK YOUR UNDERSTANDING

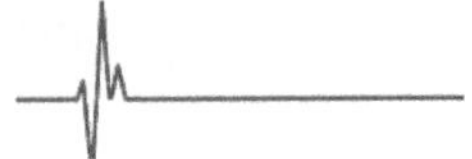

1. Your miracle is in your mouth. **(True)** **(False)**
2. Blessed are the [______] for they shall inherit the Earth (Matthew 5:5).
3. What scriptures say that God's Word is immutable and that it is impossible for Him to lie?
   (a) Mark 9:23
   (b) Numbers 23:19
   (c) Hebrews 6:18
   (d) Both B and C
4. 1 John 3:18 says, "My little children, let us not love in Word, neither in tongue, but in deed and [______]."
5. Where is this scripture found: "The Lord of hosts hath sworn, saying surely as I have thought, so shall it come to pass; and as I have purposed, so shall it stand."
   (a) Isaiah 14:24
   (b) Matthew 8:8
   (c) Psalms 17:3
6. Psalms 85:13 says, "Righteousness shall go before Him, and shall set us in the way of His steps." **(True)** **(False)**

7. What scriptures say that a liberal soul will be made fat?

   (a) Proverbs 11:25

   (b) Romans 8:28

   (c) Joshua 24:15

   (d) Genesis 1:2-3

8. Hebrews 12:2 mentions that Jesus is the author and finisher of our faith. **(True)** **(False)**

CONCLUSION

While *our words* add value to our experiences, at the end of the day it is *the Word* that changes and controls our lives. Many people are searching for answers, yearning to hear from God, longing for something they cannot explain. Truth enlightens our darkness, as a spotlight to our feet and a guiding light for the journey. The Word of God is the only sure and consistent thing that we have, in our uncertain and rapidly-changing existence. "It is the spirit that quickeneth; the flesh profiteth nothing: the words that I speak unto you, they are spirit, and they are life," (Jn. 6:63).

Incorporating positive words and godly language into our day-to-day routine, helps shift our thought patterns and actions for better. In **Chapter One: *Trouble Talk***, we discussed the consequences of damaging and discouraging conversations, and the adverse effects it can cause. Even though our moods and feelings fluctuate, the words that come out of our mouths should be stable and consistent.

In **Chapter Two: *Voice of Hope***, we find direct correlation between negative talk and sin. These corrupt traits lead an individual towards a type of spiritual prison, causing oppression, hindering blessings, and creating strongholds in our lives. Then, reading further we discover hope, and learn about how it encourages us to move forward. Hope strengthens us, and brings us peace during difficult times. No matter how hard things get, there is always something to be thankful for. Limit your bad news intake and stay encouraged. By not only possessing hope, but also speaking it into the lives of others. Doing this, we can generate resilience in God, and positivity to hold on to.

"Thou art my hiding place and my shield: I hope in thy Word," (Psa. 119:14). In conflict, you must be unafraid. Be ready to speak courageously and be willing to listen without fear. Through tribulation, patience, and experience, we invite change and can embrace new communication. Our voices are a beacon for transmission directly to Heaven. Allow God to hear your heart and get involved in your everyday situations. He has an answer for your prayer, and clarity for your decisions. "The Lord is nigh unto all them that call upon Him, to all that call upon Him in truth," (Psa. 145:18).

Reading on into **Chapter Three: *Wisdom Words***, it discusses the distinction between wisdom and knowledge. While human discernment and natural wisdom is flawed, we realize that the fear of the Lord is real wisdom. In choosing the words that we say and being mindful of what, with who, and when we speak, we can possess value in our conversations.

Later, we come to know how to recognize the voice of the Lord when He speaks to us. What God has spoken over you, your family, and your household will override every negative voice in your life. In **Chapter Four: *Speak Lord***, we went deeper into the parables of the Bible, times when the spoken Word of God commanded miracles. Jesus said "come," and Peter walked on water. Abraham "heard a voice in a bush" instructing Him not to sacrifice His son, and had supernatural provision for an offering instead. In the beginning when He said, "let there be" and light was formed and land was established, animals were multiplied and man was created, it represents the communicative power of God. That alone, shows the greatness of His power! So many instances, that reference manifested miracles simply by Him saying a word.

Over and over, scripture after scripture, it compels us to be cautious with our words. **Chapter Five: *Seasoned Speech,*** gives insight on using words of substance, and the importance of being kind and gracious in our everyday speech habits. *Even though our mouth belongs to our body, our lips are not our own.* We must watch our thoughts and constrain our words to uplift and not tear down, to heal not harm. Our talk must glorify God!

Moving into **Chapter Six: *Heart Check,*** it discusses the location of our language being a product of the condition of our hearts. Through meditation and prayer, we can cultivate Christ-like character, preventing ourselves for becoming a garbage can for 'junk and mess.' God searches our hearts, and when sin enters in, only evil words will come out.

Finally, in **Chapter Seven: *Good News*** we find that our words can be used as a positive tool to build and spread the gospel. When we speak life and say those things that we desire, we make our requests known to God, and He then can bring them to pass (Rom. 4:17). This chapter fortifies our faith, and reminds us of all the promises spoken throughout the text. From being above and not beneath, to peculiar and chosen, to a lender and not a borrower, to being able to tread on serpents and scorpions and over all the power of the enemy. *Surely, God can do it!*

Surely, God's Word is alive and purposed, uninhibited and indescribable. We must love Him without fear, and trust Him aloud. Let's choose to avoid evil communication, staying away from those who enjoy 'dangerous and deadly talking.' The *good news* is that every day is a brand-new opportunity to hope for more, to believe for greater, and to talk of His goodness. When we direct our conversations in Holiness, we can experience an unexplainable shift for good in our lives.

CALENDAR
2022

JANUARY

Sun	Mon	Tue	Wed	Thu	Fri	Sat
						1
2	3	4	5	6	7	8
9	10	11	12	13	14	15
16	17	18	19	20	21	22
23	24	25	26	27	28	29
30	31					

FEBRUARY

Sun	Mon	Tue	Wed	Thu	Fri	Sat
		1	2	3	4	5
6	7	8	9	10	11	12
13	14	15	16	17	18	19
20	21	22	23	24	25	26
27	28					

MARCH

Sun	Mon	Tue	Wed	Thu	Fri	Sat
		1	2	3	4	5
6	7	8	9	10	11	12
13	14	15	16	17	18	19
20	21	22	23	24	25	26
27	28	29	30	31		

APRIL

Sun	Mon	Tue	Wed	Thu	Fri	Sat
					1	2
3	4	5	6	7	8	9
10	11	12	13	14	15	16
17	18	19	20	21	22	23
24	25	26	27	28	29	30

MAY

Sun	Mon	Tue	Wed	Thu	Fri	Sat
1	2	3	4	5	6	7
8	9	10	11	12	13	14
15	16	17	18	19	20	21
22	23	24	25	26	27	28
29	30	31				

JUNE

Sun	Mon	Tue	Wed	Thu	Fri	Sat
			1	2	3	4
5	6	7	8	9	10	11
12	13	14	15	16	17	18
19	20	21	22	23	24	25
26	27	28	29	30		

JULY

Sun	Mon	Tue	Wed	Thu	Fri	Sat
					1	2
3	4	5	6	7	8	9
10	11	12	13	14	15	16
17	18	19	20	21	22	23
24	25	26	27	28	29	30
31						

AUGUST

Sun	Mon	Tue	Wed	Thu	Fri	Sat
	1	2	3	4	5	6
7	8	9	10	11	12	13
14	15	16	17	18	19	20
21	22	23	24	25	26	27
28	29	30	31			

SEPTEMBER

Sun	Mon	Tue	Wed	Thu	Fri	Sat
				1	2	3
4	5	6	7	8	9	10
11	12	13	14	15	16	17
18	19	20	21	22	23	24
25	26	27	28	29	30	

OCTOBER

Sun	Mon	Tue	Wed	Thu	Fri	Sat
						1
2	3	4	5	6	7	8
9	10	11	12	13	14	15
16	17	18	19	20	21	22
23	24	25	26	27	28	29
30	31					

NOVEMBER

Sun	Mon	Tue	Wed	Thu	Fri	Sat
		1	2	3	4	5
6	7	8	9	10	11	12
13	14	15	16	17	18	19
20	21	22	23	24	25	26
27	28	29	30			

DECEMBER

Sun	Mon	Tue	Wed	Thu	Fri	Sat
				1	2	3
4	5	6	7	8	9	10
11	12	13	14	15	16	17
18	19	20	21	22	23	24
25	26	27	28	29	30	31

30-DAY PRAYER JOURNAL

WHISPERERS

DANGEROUS

&

DEADLY

TALKING

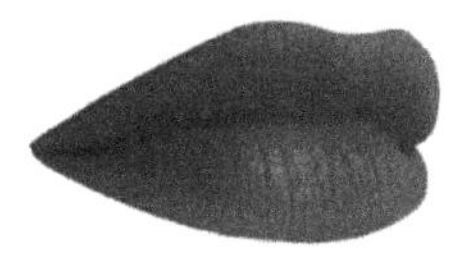

Day 1

"Call unto me, and I will answer thee, and shew thee great and mighty things, which thou knowest not." Jeremiah 33:3

Prayer: Father, hear my humble cry today. Show yourself strong in my life and handle those things too big for me to handle. You are a great God and I desire to know you more.

Day 2

"Now faith is the substance of things hoped for, the evidence of things not seen." Hebrews 11:1

Prayer: Thank you Lord for my family, my loved ones, for providing for me and protecting me. Increase my faith today and allow me to tap into the supernatural.

TO DO LIST:

AFFIRMATIONS

Day 3

"Trust in the Lord with all thine heart; and lean not unto thine own understanding." Proverbs 3:5

Prayer: God, continue to cover, lead, and guide me in all that I do. I place my trust in your Word, and have faith in your provision and promise for my life.

Day 4

"I can do all things through Christ which strengtheneth me." Philippians 4:13

Prayer: Father, thank you for strengthening me and giving me wisdom. Continue to shield me from all hurt, harm, and danger. Make me fit for the battle and able for what you have called me to do.

TO DO LIST:

AFFIRMATIONS

Day 5

"I will bless the Lord at all times: His praise shall continually be in my mouth." Psalms 34:1

Prayer: Lord, give me a heart of praise and worship. Let me exalt your name in everything that I do, that you may be glorified in me.

Day 6

"Behold, God is my salvation; I will trust, and not be afraid: for the Lord Jehovah is my strength and my song; He also is become my salvation." Isaiah 12:2

Prayer: Keep my foot from falling and my heart from being afraid. Restore my confidence in your Word and allow me to trust you on a deeper level.

TO DO LIST:

AFFIRMATIONS

Day 7

"Hatred stirreth up strifes: but love covereth all sins."
Proverbs 10:12

Prayer: Thank you Lord for allowing me to follow peace with all men and abide in Holiness. Help me to love those that hate me, and bless those that curse me.

Day 8

"O Lord, I know that the way of man is not in himself: it is not in man that walketh to direct his steps." Jeremiah 10:23

Prayer: Father, continue to guide me with your eye in the direction that I should go. Lead me in the path of righteousness for your name's sake.

AFFIRMATIONS

Day 9

"Behold, I send you forth as sheep in the midst of wolves: be ye therefore wise as serpents, and harmless as doves." Matthew 10:16

Prayer: God, give me wisdom in everything that I do, and everywhere that you send me. Open my eyes to traps, ditches, and show me every stumbling block that would hinder my path.

Day 10

"For with the heart man believeth unto righteousness; and with the mouth confession is made unto salvation." Romans 10:10

Prayer: Anoint me, from the top of my head to the soles of my feet. Allow my lips to speak of your goodness and declare your judgments. Draw me closer to you today, through your Word.

TO DO LIST:

AFFIRMATIONS

Day 11

"For who hath known the mind of the Lord, that He may instruct him? But we have the mind of Christ." 1 Corinthians 2:16

Prayer: Father, guard the gates of my mind. Give me your thoughts and allow me to think upon your Word. Instruct me on which way to go and lead me in truth.

Day 12

"This I say then, walk in the Spirit, and ye shall not fulfil the lust of the flesh." Galatians 5:16

Prayer: God, let me not be conformed to the ways of this world. Transform my inner-man so that I can walk in the Spirit and not the ways of my flesh.

TO DO LIST:

AFFIRMATIONS

Day 13

"But wilt thou know, O vain man, that faith without works is dead?" James 2:20

Prayer: Let my life be faith-filled and Holy. I want to walk, love, and move in faith. Give me supernatural vision to see beyond my reality into the promises of God.

Day 14

"I press toward the mark for the prize of the high calling of God in Christ Jesus." Philippians 3:14

Prayer: Thank you Lord for keeping my heart fixed on you. Encourage me to keep going and push me to reach for greater. I know that there are no limits in you, and your Word cannot fail.

TO DO LIST:

AFFIRMATIONS

Day 15

"As every man hath received the gift, even so minister the same one to another, as good stewards of the manifold grace of God."
1 Peter 4:10

Prayer: Father, let me go deeper in your Word. Teach me your statutes that I may do them. Soften my heart, so I can minister to others and draw them closer to you.

Day 16

"But judgment shall return unto righteousness: and all the upright in heart shall follow it." Psalms 94:15

Prayer: Thank you Lord for your judgment, that led me to deliverance. Keep me on the pathway of Holiness, and hide your Word in my heart that I may never sin against you.

TO DO LIST:

AFFIRMATIONS

Day 17

"For thou, Lord, wilt bless the righteous; with favour wilt thou compass him as with a shield." Psalms 5:12

Prayer: Father, allow favor to surround me today in the store, at school, in my home, in the car, and on my job. Show me your goodness and fill my soul with gladness.

Day 18

"I will take the cup of salvation, and call upon the name of the Lord." Psalms 116:13

Prayer: God, I call upon you today in truth. Your word says when I seek you, I will find you when I search for you with all of my heart. I am listening for your answers.

TO DO LIST:

AFFIRMATIONS

Day 19

"Rejoice in the Lord always: and again I say, Rejoice."
Philippians 4:4

Prayer: Lord, let words of joy, praise, faith, and gladness come from my lips. Strengthen my heart and give me a heart of worship today. I want my praise to be pure and true.

Day 20

"Examine yourselves, whether ye be in the faith; prove your own selves. Know ye not your own selves, how that Jesus Christ is in you, except ye be reprobates?" 2 Corinthians 13:5

Prayer: God, bring to my remembrance all that you have done for me. Allow me to recall every time you delivered and helped me, then keep me on that straight and narrow path of Holiness.

TO DO LIST:

AFFIRMATIONS

Day 21

"The Lord is my shepherd; I shall not want."
Psalms 23:1

Prayer: Lord, lead me beside the still waters and restore my soul. Fix my faith, so that I will fear no evil. Allow your rod and staff to comfort me. Allow goodness and mercy to follow me all the days of my life, and allow my cup to run over with right now prosperity.

Day 22

"Whoso offereth praise glorifieth me: and to him that ordereth his conversation aright will I shew the salvation of God." Psalms 50:23

Prayer: Father, let me speak life and not death, joy and not sorrow. Bridle my tongue when needed, and give me faith words when the time is right. I want my conversation to begin in your precepts.

TO DO LIST:

AFFIRMATIONS

Day 23

"So the workmen wrought, and the work was perfected by them, and they set the House of God in his state, and strengthened it."
2 Chronicles 24:13

Prayer: God, give me wisdom to build your house, winning souls and restoring fallen walls. Show me how to be a profit and a benefit to your Kingdom.

Day 24

"I must work the works of Him that sent me, while it is day: the night cometh, when no man can work." St. John 9:4

Prayer: Father, stir up the gifts you have placed down on the inside of me. Don't allow my hands to be weak, let me strong in carrying out the work you have called me to do.

TO DO LIST:

AFFIRMATIONS

Day 25

"The counsel of the Lord standeth for ever, the thoughts of His heart to all generations." Psalms 33:11

Prayer: Thank you Lord for loving me and guiding me. Show me the vision, continue to give my life purpose, and show me what you need me to do in these last days.

Day 26

"For with God nothing shall be impossible." Luke 1:37

Prayer: God, increase my faith today and remove all doubt from me. Give me clarity on my next move and wisdom for every decision. Blow my mind in this season, I give you the praise!

TO DO LIST:

AFFIRMATIONS

Day 27

"For by grace are ye saved through faith; and that not of yourselves: it is the gift of God: not of works, lest any man should boast." Ephesians 2:8-9

Prayer: Father, give me humble words and a meek disposition in every assignment that you have given me. Let me extend that same grace and wisdom to others.

Day 28

"Stand fast therefore in the liberty wherewith Christ hath made us free, and be not entangled again with the yoke of bondage."
Galatians 5:1

Prayer: Thank you Lord for protecting me from everything that is not like you. Align my thought, words, and desires to things of the Spirit.

TO DO LIST:

AFFIRMATIONS

Day 29

"And be not conformed to this world: but be ye transformed by the renewing of your mind, that ye may prove what is that good, and acceptable, and perfect, will of God." Romans 12:2

Prayer: God, thank you for giving me your mind. Guide every decision that I will make today and keep me in your will.

Day 30

"My mouth shall shew forth thy righteousness and thy salvation all the day; for I know not the numbers thereof" Psalms 71:15

Prayer: Teach us to number our days, that we may continually apply our hearts unto wisdom. You are soon to come back, and we want our lives, heart, words, and minds to be right before you.

TO DO LIST:

AFFIRMATIONS

ANSWER KEY:

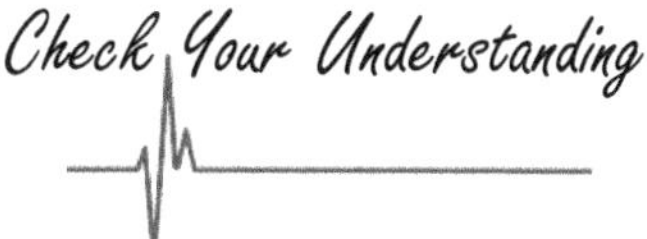

CHAPTER ONE

1 – True

2 – Romans 1:28-32

3 – A

4 – Tongue

5 – 1 Peter 3:4

6 – Proverbs 21:23

7 – Cursings

CHAPTER TWO

1 – True

2 – Deceit, Cunning, Sly, Double-Dealing

3 – C

4 –Perfection on the Cross; Jesus

5 – C

6 – B

7 – True

8 – False; You

9 – Cheap

10 – Video or Virtual Game; Levels

CHAPTER THREE

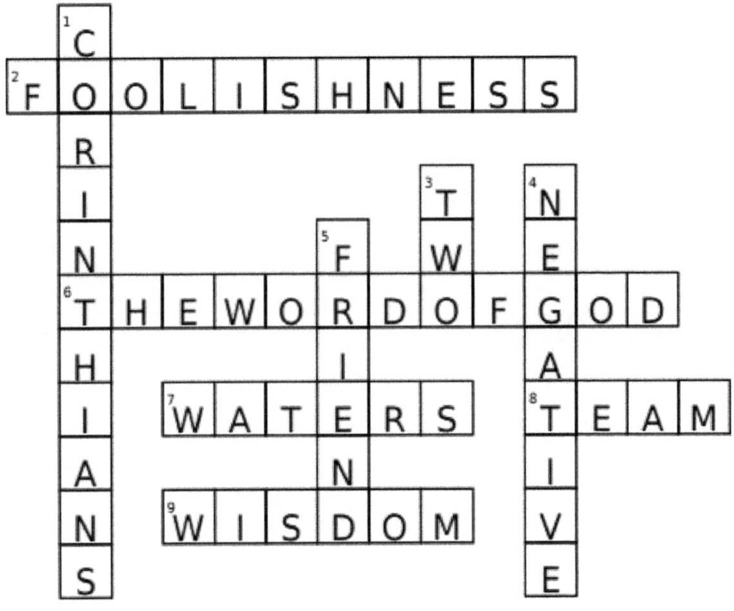

CHAPTER FOUR

1 – True

2 – Portion

3 – D

4 – Settles

5 - B

6 – Justified; Condemned

CHAPTER FIVE

1 – True

2 – Voice

3 – A

4 – Heart

5 – B

6 – True

CHAPTER SIX

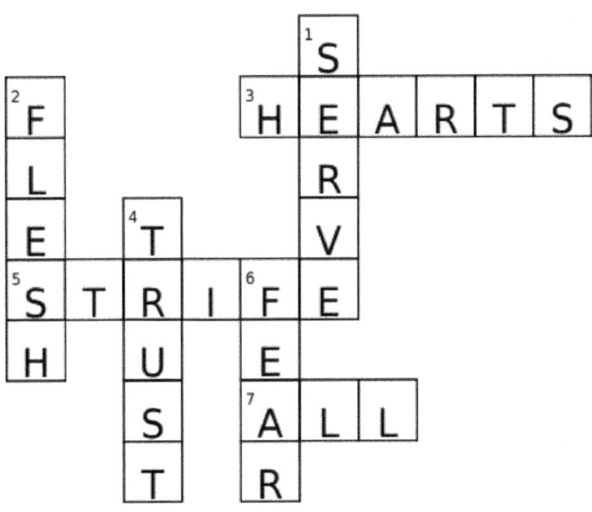

CHAPTER SEVEN

1 – True

2 – Meek

3 – D

4 – Truth

5 – A

6 – True

7 - A

8 - True

ABOUT THE AUTHOR

BISHOP M.B. JEFFERSON is an innovative leader and an instrumental asset to the body of Christ. With his fiery testimony and prophetic gifting, he has influenced a world-wide awakening for truth. Through messages of Jesus Christ, Bishop Jefferson impacts the lives of thousands of individuals across the globe. In his call for change, he continues to spread messages of hope and holiness, to all with a hearing ear and a desire for deliverance.

For over forty-plus years in ministry, Bishop M.B. Jefferson and his wife, Dr. Brenda Jefferson have remained faithful to the call of God on their lives. They are founders and senior pastors of Living in Victory Christian Church, The House of David Help Center, M.B. Jefferson Ministries, and World Assemblies Fellowship International. Through scripture-based teachings, they uniquely point believers and non-believers alike toward the cross. Teaching love, judgment, kindness, and the harmful effects of addiction and sin. Many lives have been changed through their ministry.

OTHER WORKS BY AUTHOR

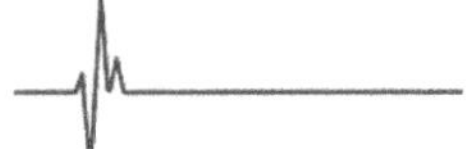

THOUGHT WATCHERS

CHANGE YOUR THOUGHTS, CHANGE YOUR WORLD

LIVING IN VICTORY

TRANSFORMATION OF THE MIND

THE 50 LIST

I GOT IT

VISIT BISHOP MB JEFFERSON ONLINE:

You Tube Channel: Bishop MB Jefferson

Instagram: MBJeffersonMin

www.mbjefferson.org

www.livcc.org

CPSIA information can be obtained
at www.ICGtesting.com
Printed in the USA
LVHW080440100222
710546LV00002B/15